Poet, Mystic, Modern Hero
Fernando Rielo Pardal

Scripta Humanistica

Directed by
BRUNO M. DAMIANI
The Catholic University of America

ADVISORY BOARD

Poet, Mystic, Modern Hero
Fernando Rielo Pardal

Zelda Irene Brooks

𝔖𝔠𝔯𝔦𝔭𝔱𝔞 ℌ𝔲𝔪𝔞𝔫𝔦𝔰𝔱𝔦𝔠𝔞
79

Brooks, Zelda Irene.
    Poet, mystic, modern hero: Fernando Rielo Pardal / by Zelda
Irene Brooks.
        p. cm. -- (Scripta Humanistica; 79)
    Includes bibiliographical references.
    ISBN 0-916379-85-X : $49.50
    1. Rielo, Fernando, 1923- --Criticism and interpretation.
2. Mysticism in literature. I. Title. II. Series: Scripta
Humanistica (Series); 79.
PQ6668.I537Z55   1991
861' . 64--dc20   91-11516
                                                 CIP

Publisher and Distributor:
SCRIPTA HUMANISTICA
1383 Kersey Lane
Potomac, Maryland 20854 U.S.A.

Printed in the United States of America

This Book is dedicated to my syster,
Carol Suzanne Brooks

Fernando Rielo Pardal
Drawing by Leif Kvammen

Table Of Contents

Note From The Author

I have translated Fernando Rielo's exquisitely beautiful Spanish verse simply out of a desire to make available to those who do not read Spanish a fundamental sense of his poetry. I personally know many of his admirers who do not read Spanish and this has given me the courage to undertake this endeavor. Brackets represent the mark of my translations. Some quotes in prose from Spanish critics do not include the original Spanish. I have done all my own translations in order to present a consistent style. At times I felt intimidated, particularly when working with the poet's splendid sonnets where the English can only approach Rielo's mastery. Only their extraordinary lyric quality, the synthesis of symbol and theme, subdued my doubts and encouraged me to complete the project.

Eugene Nida, one of the foremost translators of the Bible, uses the term "dynamic equivalence" to define the tension inherent in a good translation. "Dynamic" favors the contextually appropriate target language, while "equivalent" stresses faithfulness to the original. Excess in the direction of dynamic renders only paraphrase, but excess towards equivalence can present an unnaturally literal, sometimes lifeless version. Translating mystical poetry from a language with a tradition of special symbols required more attention to equivalence. Because of the different system of values, as well as the different perspective of reality in the ancient words of Spanish mysticism, the translation is almost literal. And still, the original contains complex concepts, history and myth that cannot be fully rendered in English. Hopefully, the interpretative material of the text will make some of that clearer, but several volumes would have to be written to cover the breadth of language in this tradition.

Moreover, the power of the octasyllabic Spanish meter and the Spanish sonnet cannot be duplicated when translated into English. Equally elusive is Rielo's keen sense of the symbolic and psychological value in the interplay of "mystical words", a reinvention of language born of his genius. In spite of these limitations, I hope the pursuit of "dynamic equivalence" reflects my devotion to the poet and provides assistance to the English reader.

Foreword

In ancient times, the term "Hero" referred to a man who watched over, a man who protected, a watchman. In the legends of mythology a hero was a man of great strength and courage, favored by the gods and in part descended from them. He was often regarded as a half-god and was worshipped after his death. Today a hero is simply a man admired for his courage, nobility, and achievements. (Webster)

Fernando Rielo is a modern hero and a living legend of the twentieth century. Few men in history have dedicated the whole of their energy, faith and devotion to the common good of mankind; Rielo is one of those men. His life's goal is a better world, a just and compassionate society, and his extraordinary strength and courage have enabled him to take important steps toward reaching that goal. He has established himself as an international civic and religious leader, having founded, to date (1990), centers and hospitals in eighteen nations in Latin America, North America, Europe, Africa, and the Middle East.

His efforts as a thinker and writer have produced masterpieces in various genres including philosophy, the essay, mystic poetry, proverbs, and literary criticism. His literary contributions have been highly praised by such respected critics and poets such as Dámaso Alonso, Jean Claude Renard, Zamora Vicente, Claude Couffon, García Nieto, Jaime Ferrán, Odón Betanzos, and Gazarian-Gautier.

Among the many titles of honor that belong to Fernando Rielo that of educator must be included. His philosophy, poetry, and other writings reveal the heart of a true educator who communicates with his readers on both cultural and personal levels and who challenges their

1

analytical skills. His insights open horizons onto new and expanded possibilities and values. Moral education and ethics assume their proper elevated position not only in his writings but also in the institutions that he has founded. Particularly important in this respect is the *Escuela Idente*, an international school that strives to teach young people to become citizens of the world, and to think clearly and thoroughly with deep understanding of the varied dimensions of moral and spiritual values. Drawing students and teachers together in a shared exploration of issues, Rielo's *Escuela Idente* engages in actual moral education, and develops in its students the characteristics of integrity, honesty, trustworthiness, courage, love, and the capacity to think for themselves. They are taught how to think, not what to think.

Fernando Rielo Pardal was born to Enrique and Pilar on the 28th of August in 1923 in Madrid, Spain. He spent his childhood in Madrid during difficult years of conflict and danger. His studies at the *Real Instituto de San Isidro* were interrupted by the Civil War. However, when the fighting was over he completed his studies there. He served for a brief period as a career officer, but a spiritual awakening changed his life abruptly and he began the studies in theology and philosophy which were to be his destiny. In 1957 he moved to Santa Cruz de Tenerife, the Spanish territory of the Canary Islands. In 1958 he published his first book of mystic poems called *Dios y árbol* [God and Tree].

In the preface to this first book of exquisite lyrical verse in the mystical tradition, Rielo explains to readers the fundamental meaning of his poetry:

Its meaning is that of a symbol, destiny, addressed to mankind as a whole; a destiny in which all men and women are forever installed. The theme of my poetry is destiny itself. Someone is the Absolute Subject of our loving destiny that even death cannot close. ("A la atención del lector", *Dios y árbol* 5)

This same preface clearly delineates Rielo's mystical vision of man as god, as hero--a vision derived from the aforementioned tradition of mythical legend:

I offer you, in summary, an image of God as the illustrious form of our destiny and of that which you are as a human being his tree; a tree that is at the same time a God. I suppose you thus in my poetry, dear reader, as the deity you are and never less than that. (5)

This vision is grounded in the authority of Scripture by means of an allusion to John 10:33-6, where Jesus uses the term "gods" to describe those "unto whom the word of God came."[1]

Throughout Rielo's career, this vision has found expression not only in poetry but also in educational and civic work. In Tenerife in 1959, this vision led Rielo to found a Catholic institute of higher education, *Fundacion de Cristo Redentor e Instituto Id: Misioneros y misioneras Identes* [The Foundation of Christ the Redeemer and *Id* Institute: *Idente* Missionaries]. The majority of missionaries, who are members of this foundation, now extended throughout many nations, hold the Ph.D in both theology and philosophy as well as in a third field of specialization which varies according to individual talent and interest. Those fields include law, engineering, medicine, biology, chemistry, physics, pedagogy and literature among others. Fernando Rielo is affectionately called *Nuestro Padre Fundador* [Our Founding Father] by the extraordinarily talented and committed *Idente* missionaries. They live together in communities and respond to their founder's call: *Id. Id* is the plural imperative of the Spanish verb for *to go*: "Go forth" and heal the sick; feed the poor; educate the youth of the world in the humanities, the sciences, and the love of God. This is the mandate of the founding father and these are the life-tasks of his missionaries who could be called priests and sisters of the highest Catholic tradition. They continually renew their vows of poverty, chastity, and faith; they commit their lives to the service of God not only in prayer and liturgical practices but in active work in international education and health centers and parishes around the world. They take a special vow of academic excellence in order to prepare themselves academically and professionally to defend Christian ideals, the Catholic Church, and the honorable head of the Church in the person of Pope.

---

1. The full text of John 10:33-6 reads as follows: "The Jews answered him, saying, For a good work we stone thee not; but for blasphemy; and because that thou, being a man, makest thyself God. Jesus answered them. Is it not written in your law, I said, Ye are gods? If he called them gods, unto whom the word of God came, and the scripture cannot be broken; say ye of him, whom the father hath sanctified, and sent into the world, thou blasphemeth; because I said, I am the Son of God?"

3

Each of the Foundation Centers has weekly cultural events or athenaeums, usually on Sunday, when doors are open to the community and all may participate creatively in the writing and performing or reading of mystic poetry, music, drama, and philosophy. These events maintain the high standards of integrity, love and faith of the missionaries who have dedicated their lives to God.

Fernando Rielo's missionaries are united in their love of Jesus Christ as "the way, the truth and the life." Their purpose is to assist the international youth of today in reaching their full moral and spiritual, as well as intellectual, potential. They are modern day apostles who go forth to live and practice and teach the word of God wherever the Church might need them, dedicating to their institutions and congregations the ecumenical commitment of the founders of the Catholic Church.

Rielo's civic and educational projects also include the *Juventud Idente* [Idente Youth], a group whose goal is to draw together the highest cultural and moral ideals of the youth of many different countries, races, and beliefs in order to form a "universal parliament of youth." In addition, Rielo has recently founded a health association in Rome: *Asociación Sanitaria Fernando Rielo*. This foundation provides medical and civil assistance to the immigrants there.

Such civic, educational, and religious projects, however, have by no means diminished--indeed, have only strengthened--Rielo's commitment both to his personal literary vocation and to the encouragement of important literature worldwide. In 1978 Rielo published *Llanto azul* [Blue Sob], his most widely acclaimed book of mystic poetry. The following years were also intensively dedicated to poetry. In 1979 *Paisaje desnudo* [Naked Landscape] and *Pasión y muerte* [Passion and Death], two outstanding volumes of mystic poetry, were published, and in 1980 another in the classical mystic tradition called *Noche clara* [Clear Night].

By 1981, Rielo's intense passion for poetry and the arts brought about the founding of a cultural organization bearing his name: the Fernando Rielo Foundation. This foundation is a nonprofit organization recognized by the Spanish government that seeks to promote encounters among different traditions and cultures in Spain and internationally. In keeping with Rielo's personal humanistic aims and endeavors the principal aim of the foundation is the development of humane values and the promotion of literature, especially mystic poetry, as well as of all the other arts at an international level.

The main activities of the Fernando Rielo Foundation are divided into different fields such as poetry, music, pedagogy, and philosophy, though it remains open to additions from other fields that might arise in the course of its ongoing work. Specifically, the Foundation organizes poetry readings, concerts, lectures, courses and other events, as well as sponsoring a diverse array of publishing projects. It also initiates and organizes gatherings that draw together literary, musical, and philosophical activities, and it participates actively in congresses and exhibitions at the local, national, and international level. The headquarters of the Foundation is in Madrid, but it maintains delegations in fifteen countries and collaborates with a large number of highly trained professionals who assist in all phases of organization and work. It has close ties with other foundations and organizations in Spain and around the world, and it actively pursues joint projects with various embassies and universities, as well as with UNESCO.

The section of the Fernando Rielo Foundation dedicated to poetry promotes poetic production as an expression of the profound sensibility possible in mankind in the face of a transcendent reality--a reality which as we have already seen, Rielo believes to be man's essential destiny. Poetry, according to this conception, can open the doors and initiate constructive dialogue between races, cultures, and differing constructions of reality; the fruit of poetry is peace. As Rielo puts it:

Man, the heir of opposing forces, when faced with peace and nonpeace, has not succeeded in choosing precisely what defines peace: poetry. I am referring to the great poetry of life and not at all to rhetoricized language lacking those spiritual values which are proper to the human soul. Peace is single, necessary, indivisible. Poetry is its richest language because it possesses a multiform world of images which movingly recreate our feelings.

In homage to this exalted conception of poetry, the Fernando Rielo Foundation includes within its program for the promotion of poetry the publication of the plurilingual international poetry journal *Equivalences*. This international literary journal is directed by the prestigious Spanish poet Justo Jorge Padrón, recipient this year of the Crown of Gold Poetry Prize of the International Poetry Festival held

5

at Struga, Yugoslavia. The journal focuses on current, unpublished poetry and has included contributions from internationally renowned poets and essayists such as Octavio Paz, Allen Ginsberg, Rafael Alberti, Léopold Sédar Senghor, and Jon Silkin, and Jorge Guillen to name but a few. The journal also seeks out young, still undiscovered poets whose talents warrant an international forum. Thus far *Equivalences* has attracted contributions from more than 120 poets representing such diverse nations as the United States, Spain, Yugoslavia, Malta, Rumania, Mexico, France, Germany, England, Scotland, Italy, Argentina, Chile, Perú, Colombia, Portugal, Belgium, and Nicaragua.

Equivalences employs an experienced team of translators, providing its readers with a completely bilingual Spanish-English text on facing pages, in addition to the native tongues of poets representing other language communities. The journal's high standards of content and format render it unique in international publishing. University circles are acclaiming its value for teaching comparative literature and linguistics as well as literary translation in the standard languages and the less commonly taught languages. The special recognition that this literary journal has been given by the academic community render it a necessary item for any public or private library concerned with contemporary poetry.

The publishing activities of the foundation are also responsible for the collection of contemporary Hispanic texts of the mystical tradition in poetry titled the *Sky Blue Collection*. This series includes poems awarded the World Prize for Mystical Poetry as well as those which, for their special literary value or as contributions to man's perennial heritage, deserve to be made available to interested readers.

The Fernando Rielo World Prize for Mystical Poetry [*Premio Mundial de Poesía Mística*] is given once a year; it consists of 600,000 pesetas (approximately $6,000) and the publication of the winning entry. Rielo intends this prize to encourage a growing sensitivity to the celestial transcendence of the human spirit in the face of the materialism which powerfully conditions much contemporary thought and cultural production. The prerequisite for winning this prize is a demonstrated mastery of heightened spirituality in the context of authentic literary creation. Its ethical substance involves a poet's expression of his "condition" or "elevated state of being" as an implicit declaration of his state of "being in love" with God. Even works which do not precisely fulfill these particularly difficult requirements, however, may still be considered for the award, as Rielo makes clear:

The stringency of this model should, however be tempered by human understanding and openness enabling the prize to be awarded to poets who, though distinguished more for their literary creativity than for their mystical wealth, contribute a sensibility worthy of respect. This prize is rooted in a mystical principle: to manage when the desired goal was not fulfilled, to give the prize, before declaring it void of a winner, to true poets who, although they cannot be classified as mystics in terms of a typical definition, nevertheless dream buried [*sepultados*] in a datum essential to art: the mystery of suffering is the poet's companion.

This prize does not discriminate by sex, age, nationality or race. The foundation that awards it actively supports women's rights and recognition in the arts. In 1982, for example, the World Prize for Mystical Poetry was awarded to Blanca Andreu for her book *Báculo de Babel* [Babel Staff]; Andreu's importance and influence in contemporary Spanish literature was confirmed that same year when whe received the ADONIS prize for poetry, Spain's most prestigious poetry award, for her book *De una niña de provincia que se vino a vivir en un chagal* [Of a provincial girl who came to live in a Chagall]. Rielo's statement about the Mystical Poetry Prize's recognition of "the mystery of suffering" is borne out by Andreu's description of *Babel Staff* in a pamphlet from the IV European Congress of Poetry in Louvain as "a long poem, a delirium written in two days and originally intended to be a letter for a certain person. There is mention of love, of solitude; I try to subject the dispersion of languages-hence the title- and submerge myself in identity, in my own internal chaos...." (n. pag.)

Other cultural activities of the Fernando Rielo Foundation include the International Institute of Music, designed to teach Pianistic techniques under the direction of the celebrated professor Américo Caramuta; the Seminar on Thought, initiated with a seminar on Spanish thought; prizes for foreign students in cooperation with diplomatic missions; and courses and awards in collaboration with UNESCO for young people from countries other than Spain studying Spanish language and literature. The Foundation works intensively to bring foreign artists into Spain and also to promote Spanish authors in other countries.

Through the Fernando Rielo Foundation and through the publication of his own poetry (the latest volumes being *Balcón a la bahía* [Balcony on the Bay], 1989, and *Dolor entre cristales* [Pain within Panes], 1990, Rielo has done much to make a wide range of important literary work available to the general public. In contrast, however, his voluminous writings on philosophy are largely still unpublished and thus unavailable to a wide audience. This is doubly unfortunate since, as I will show in a later chapter, Rielo's philosophical thought undoubtedly marks an important turning point in the history of philosophy in general and is unprecedented in Spanish philosophical writings to date. His most important contribution as a writer in terms of revolutionary thought and in sheer volume is in the field of philosophy. He has written some 200 volumes of philosophy which are only now coming to press. His genetic concept of metaphysics has been examined and debated at several international conferences of the United Nations, the Organization of American States, and UNESCO as well as at various universities and cultural centers in the United States, France, Italy, and Spain. Some of the titles of the papers presented at these conferences include the following: "Concepción mística del hombre" ["Mystical Conception of Man"]; "Teoría estética" ["Aesthetic Theory"]; "Concepción genética del infinito" ["Genetic Conception of the Infinite"]; "Plateresco, mensaje inédito" ["Plateresque, Unpublished Message"]; "Ser y verdad" ["Being and Truth"]; "Concepción genética de la metafísica" ["Genetic Conception of Metaphysics"]; "Concepción genética de la ética" ["Genetic Conception of Ethics"]; "Concepción genética del derecho" ["Genetic Conception of Law"]; "Teología metafísica" ["Metaphysical Theology"]; and "Teología Física" ["Physical Theology"]. Rielo's critical studies on the principles of identity, metaphysics, and logic are compiled in a manuscript titled "Crítica a los sistemas filosóficas y escuelas teológicas" ["Critique of Philosophical Systems and Theological Schools."] Other manuscripts include studies of various disciplines viewed from the perspective of genetic metaphysics. His latest philosophical contribution, published in 1990, sprang from the meetings of the *Aula de Pensamiento* of the Fernando Rielo Foundation. Titled *Existe una filosofía española? Raíces y valores históricos del pensamiento español* [Is There a Spanish Philosophy? Roots and Historic Values of Spanish Thought], it provides a synthesis of Fernando Rielo's philosophic thought in a single volume.

One of Rielo's most original ideas is found in a collection of his essays called *Teoría del Quijote: Su mística hispánica* now found in

English translation as *Theory of Don Quijote: Its Hispanic Mysticism*. As the title suggests, Rielo argues in these essays that the *Ingenioso Hidalgo Don Quijote de la Mancha* represents the passage of Spanish mysticism into the novel. Although the verbal and stylistic brilliance of these essays (and especially the innovative metaphysical and mystical terms they deploy) would alone suffice to make them a masterpiece of literary criticism, their most important contribution lies in their vision of Spain and its cultural projection into the world. Rielo not only examines Quijotism but presents a vision of the essence of Don Quijote as manifested throughout Hispanic literature and culture. He goes beyond Quijote by means of a literary intervention which brings to life the significance of Spanish cultural values. This intervention consists in a convincing revelation of mysticism as the keynote to the interpretation of Hispanic culture. What is the core, the heart of Spanish culture? For the answer to this question, Rielo argues, one must turn to the mystics and, more specifically, to the *Quijote* as a mystical novel.

The innovative force and importance of Rielo's recently translated study of Cervantes, especially for English-language readers, can be gauged by placing it in the context of the overall range of Cervantes criticism available in English. First, one is forced to conclude that the axiom with which the Cambridge guide to the *Literature of the Spanish People* begins its Cervantes chapter--"A curious thing about Spanish literature is that it travels badly" (175)--applies doubly to Spanish criticism in English. For aside from the work of Salvador de Madariaga and Savi López, much of the most important Spanish criticism of Cervantes remains untranslated, including Menéndez Pidal's *Cervantes y Lope de Vega*, Juan Arbo's *Cervantes*, and works by José María Asensio y Toledo and Manuel Azaña. Second, critical studies in English are relatively few in number, and many are outdated.[2] Furthermore, such studies tend to focus on somewhat peripheral topics, such as customs, stylistics, how to teach Cervantes, the author's

2. Much of the English-language work on Cervantes was done decades ago, with the result that most of it is out of print. See Bell, Bernadete and Flores, Entwhistle, Ford and Lansing, and Grisner. Happily, works by Schevill, Watts, and Fitzmaurice-Kelly have been reprinted. However, H.R. Hays' translation of Juan Ramón Jiménez essays does not include Cervantes in its selection from Jiménez portraits of writers. More recent English-language studies include Church, Close, Green, Mosely, Torbert, and Wilson. One should also note the Cervantes Society of America's journal <u>Cervantes</u>.

feminist sensibilities, and even such things as place-names. The Cambridge and the Chandler and Schwartz histories of Spanish literature devote a good deal of space to Cervantes' absurdist wit, revolutionary psychology, and taming of what they take to be innate Spanish fanaticism. Treating *Don Quixote* as a wonderful travelogue of seventeenth-century Spain, they document Cervantes' sketchy education and deep knowledge of the common people, considering him an ordinary man who became a sort of social critic. They call *Don Quijote* the "tragedy of reformers" and document its power as a chronicle of moral education.

As my use of the term "document" suggests, the major problem with most English-language works on Cervantes and *Don Quijote* is that they treat both author and character not as what Benedetto Croce would have called "monuments," but rather as "documents," as measurements or milestones of something else. Furthermore, I have not found a single work dealing with the mysticism of Cervantes. The only mention that the Cambridge history makes is negative, calling *Don Quijote* an "epistemological riddle ... without a trace of mysticism" (191). Chandler and Schwartz devote many pages to mysticism, mostly the Siglo de Oro classics such as Fray Luis de León, San Juan de la Cruz, and Santa Teresa de Jesús, but Cervantes is conspicuously absent from those pages.

The exceptional value and importance of Rielo's *Theory of Don Quijote* thus lies in its tracing a fundamental and historically constant core of mysticism through all the various dimensions of Hispanic culture as well as through that culture's historical evolution. The study follows the course of Spanish mystical thought from its most remote origins in the *Devotio Iberica* [a sacred oath for life in favor of the other members of the community]; through the Silver Age of the Visigoths, as exmplified by St. Isidore; and into the Golden Age of the famed Spanish mystics Santa Teresa and San Juan de la Cruz to sct the parameters for an original interpretation of *Don Quijote*.

As this brief survey of his career shows, Fernando Rielo's civic and educational projects, his art, his critical studies, and his philosophy form a harmonious unity. There is no division, no fragmentation. We see in Don Rielo a true modern hero, a man who balances perfectly the concerns of heart, mind, body, and spirit. His life itself is unitive, inclusive, and expansive. He has not isolated himself behind the walls of his own competitive desires and achievements. Rather, his work in all fields forms a continuing expression of his love of mankind, nature, the universe, and God--the love mirrored in his extraordinary poetry. That poetry's radical challenge: the possibility of a world without brutality, hatred, violence, misery, and confusion. The new world envisioned in that poetry--a world where love *is*, where compassion *is*--constitutes Rielo's gift to the reader. Creating such a world, as Rielo's poetry shows, involves entering into the root meaning of passion as sorrow. Poetic movement begins with sorrow; the sorrow is embraced and absorbed until it turns into passion and passion in turn becomes love. In this Rielo's thought parallels the thought of Eckhardt, the German mystic: "God is in all things. He is the light that shines when the veil is rent." Or as Rielo himself puts it, "Si quieres llegar a sabio, detente en el misterio que tú eres" ["If you wish to become wise, dwell upon the mystery you are"]; (*Transfigurations* 84). Fernando Rielo is not only a modern hero; he is also the Prince from the ancient fairy tale who has come into his own and the door is shut; he works his magic.

I

Poetry As Communication

To establish the setting of the present study let us begin with a passage from a poem collected in Fernando Rielo's 1990 volume *Dolor entre cristales* [*Pain within Panes*]. Written and set in New York City, this poem explores the problems faced by poetry as a communicative act in the contemporary social world:

[The sky in New York rain of planes
kidnapped by stars and truths;
it seems like a Hollywood movie:
each plane an actor with makeup.

And why go further than Earth
if the moon has its banner?
the moon will fall too at the end of the world
dragging scenery before it.

The fall of those idols of sky
concludes that death is worth nothing:
not even the vile price of a dollar
that an absent-minded man finds in his pothole.

This sunset of the sky on our earth
is premonition of the fleeting instant
that velocity can neither wash nor extinguish:
only space and its air subsist.

Technology cannot reach my soul
although stars and galaxy reach:
my only star is much, much farther
with her invisible step of lover wing.

Only I know it because it is mine:
You gave me a 6th of January, Father
that star that guided the Three Wise Men
and that dries my sob in this valley

It goes out on me it is true, sometimes
and appears again incessant light
when pain reaches my lament
and in breathed love I continue my travel...

How to exclaim that technology and Creation
are distant from the invulnerable end
of my destiny in perfumed sob
that now no longer sheds tear nor blood?

Then I will be bird of your happiness
and in my feathers you will see your blue semblance:
this hour, finally, will recreate the intactile
kiss for that which You, Father, created me.]

El cielo en Nueva York lluvia de aviones
por secuestro de estrellas y verdades;
parece una película de Hollywood:
cada avión, un actor con maquillaje.

¿para qué ir más lejos de la tierra
si la luna tiene su estandarte?
caerá también la luna al fin del mundo
arrastrando escenario por delante.

La caída de estos ídolos del cielo
concluye que la muerte nada vale:
ni siquiera el precio ínfimo de un dólar
que un hombre despistado halla en un bache.

Este ocaso del cielo en nuestra tierra
premonición es del fugaz instante
que la velocidad ni ase ni extingue:
sólo subsisten el espacio y su aire.

La técnica no puede alcanzar mi alma
aunque estrellas y pléyades alcance:
mi estrella única está mucho más lejos
con su invisible paso de ala amante.

Sólo yo la conozco porque es mía:
Tú me la diste un seis de enero, Padre,
esa estrella que guió a los Reyes Magos
y que enjuga mi llanto en este valle.

Se me apaga, es verdad, algunas veces
y aparece otra vez luz incesante
cuando llega el dolor a mi lamento
y en aspirado amor sigo mi viaje..

¿Cómo exclamar que técnica y creación
son ajenas al fin invulnerable
de mi destino en perfumado llanto
que ya no vierte lágrima ni sangre?

Entonces seré ave de tu dicha
y en mis plumas verás tu azul semblante:
esta hora, al fin, recreará el intáctil
beso para el que Tú, Padre, me creaste.   (24-25)

This study will begin by examining the problem of the communicability of poetry, specifically the elements poetry must embody in order to become a common mode of expression and lose once and for all its limited use as idiom for initiates, a sacred but unfortunately dead language. Fernando Rielo is a mystic poet and philosopher of a particular time and place--here, now, in a world where an interest in poetic endeavors may appear quite insignificant to certain minds. Many of us doubt the seriousness of poetic activity, perhaps because of the overwhelming force of contemporary social and political realities: war, drugs, pollution, crime, environmental death threats, nuclear war. To allow oneself in these days the luxury of sitting before a sheet of paper, as Unamuno puts it, to sing of the thighs of a passing mistress, or to repeat the *carpe diem*, seems a childishness so outrageous that, lacking irony, simple modesty would suffice to stop us. We find ourselves in a position *sous rature*, as Derridá so cleverly puts it, complicit as we are in the universal confusion, misery, and crimes of our century. The "communion" that we cannot attain in the harmony of mutual ideals is being attained instead in universal suffering, which drags us into mutual ruin. This seems to be the nature of our current human condition, our place in the sun, our moment of truth, as the Spanish say.

In Fernando Rielo's poetics the love of God is the force that creates in the poet a passion for language and the need to surpass onself through artistic expression, to create universal values. At the same time, Rielo's verse reveals clearly its roots in those situations where the pressure of history is the most compelling, that is, in the common suffering of mankind, in mankind's desperate, even fatal attempts to find fulfillment and peace. In Rielo's mystical verse God is the Father, God is love, God is spirit, God is power and eternal life. He is not only the Supreme Being who created all things, but he loves and enlightens and becomes all things to those who believe, those who "feel Him to be Father":

> [Son, I am for you
> God, Father, Friend
> and son if you ask me
> I am your beloved
> and your lover. You
> tell me so. If you feel me to be
> Father, everything is yours: my kingdom
> my throne
> and I myself.]

> Hijo, soy para ti
> Dios, Padre, Amigo
> e Hijo si me lo pides.
> Soy tu amado
> y tu amante. Tú
> me lo dices. Si me sientes
> Padre, todo es tuyo: mi reino,
> mi trono
> y yo mismo.
>> ("Hijo," *Llanto azul* 30)

These qualities of God become very personal for Rielo. He expresses his experience of God not through abstactions like heaven, but through such immediately sensuous images as "kisses round as a ball":

[Now I give you not heaven;
yes a kiss round as a ball
that entertains the child
empty and all so it won't weigh him down.]

Ahora te doy, no el cielo;
si un beso redondo como pelota
que al niño entretiene,
hueca y todo para que no le pese.   (30)

This personalizing quality of Rielo's mysticism is one of its most moving features. Tenderness, gentleness, and compassion flow from his verse. God's all-encompassing power and wisdom are couched in terms of love and compassion with just a hint of levity:

[Remember my comings and goings
to bring you tiny breeze wings
that I dressed you in and the angels
kept shouting:

                    a little bird
                    in sight!

They were mistaken, because they knew nothing
of our games. How much
I laughed with them
in your first days
when you didn't even know how to speak.
Yes to paint birds.
I taught you.
And you made many
that I would give life;
and they flew

forming paradises
that you would live in a few moments,
a few moments, yes...

Larger
than life!

No. You can't remember
how many there were,
how many are the birds
that were born of our kisses.
never mind, son
I tell you that not even one
has died.

All of them
are
there!]

¿Recuerdas mis idas y venidas
para traerte alitas de brisa
que yo te ponía y los ángeles
gritaban:

¡un avecilla
a la vista!

Erraban, porque nada sabían
de nuestros juegos. Cuánto
me reí con ellos
en tus días primeros
que ni hablar sabías.
Sí pintar aves.
Yo te enseñé.
Y muchas hiciste
que yo daba la vida;

y ellas volaban
formando paraísos
que tú habitabas unos instantes,
unos istantes, sí...

¡más grandes
que la vida!

No. No puedes recordar
cuántas fueron,
cuántas son las aves
que con nuestros besos nacieron.
no importa, hijo
Yo te digo que ninguna
ha muerto.

¡Todas
están
ahí!   (31-33)

The power of Rielo's technique lies in its perfect blending of form and content with the perspective or persona of the voice of God speaking to man, much as Nietzsche records "Life" speaking to Zarathustra in that beautiful poem "The Second Dance Song." This particular technique allows the feeling of deep compassion to be imaged metaphorically and symbolically.

God tells his children that He will become even their son, that, in other words, He will become Christ. In the son is found the full manifestation of all of God's love, light, spirit, and truth. The Beyond or God is thus manifested in the world of man, in man himself, if he but awakens to it. The last verse of the preceding poem makes that idea clear:

[Wake up to the world
for the world is yours
even if it doesn't seem to be,
Yes. Life, Peace and glory
that you hope for of me

                     now
                     is...
                     your crown!]

        Despierta al mundo
        que el mundo es tuyo,
        aunque no parezca
        sí. La vida, la paz y la gloria
        que de mí esperas

                     !ya
                     es...
                     tu corona!   (33)

    This is the essence of Rielo's Christian mystic experience: unity
with God; God in man; man in God. Or, as Jesus' words in the Gospel
of John put it, "That they may all be one, even as thou, Father art in me,
and I in thee" (John 17:21). The revealing lines "wake up to the world
/ for the world is yours" illustrate Rielo's position. Man can enter into
this unity with God if his consciousness is awakened. And man *is* the
world; thus his responsibility is individual and immediate.

    Belief in magic, miracle, and the power of the word seems to have
disappeared; those forces no longer seem to inspire widespread faith.
Concurrently, the moral value of language and its potential for creating
examples of moral action have faded. For Rielo the struggle to restore
the moral value of language, and the consequent perception of truth
or reality, constitues a primary objective. He is not content to meddle
with unexpected metamorphoses or imaginary marvels; nor does he
intend merely to reveal to the reader the deep recesses of the "poetic
experience," mystic or otherwise, or to "liberate" words from their
ordinary sense. Although one could argue that his verse in fact does
all of these things, its primary, overriding objective is the revelation of
a verity that is true for all, a verity that often escapes logical
formulation.

    Fernando Rielo takes responsibility for language and its moral
value, and this responsibility requires him to preserve, to search out,
and to expand the common meaning of words that reflect concrete
experience that even the humblest reader recognizes as real. This is
particularly true of the second phase of his poetry, written after 1980.

Yet, paradoxically, Rielo's poetry also operates on an esoteric[1] level accessible only to the few; indeed, the esoteric dimension of his poetry has provided the basis for many highly sophisticated critical studies. This paradoxical combination of common and esoteric levels of meaning stems from Rielo's technique of making words become symbol that enter the reader's perception through both emotional and intellectual avenues. Words as symbol become limpid in Rielo's verse and are read and understood in accordance with the principles of Heideggerian "forestructure," or, moving one step further, in accordance with the reader's level of being and consciousness. Since his writing is a consciously produced act of creativity, that is, an act through which the writer strives to attain a state of higher consciousness, it holds the capacity to produce change in the reader: change in thought, change in feeling, and, most significantly, change in understanding.

When questions arise as to the value of poetry, and particularly mystical poetry, in an age confronted by hunger, oppression, death, crime, drugs, acid rain, ozone destruction, and the threat of nuclear war as daily conditions, the answer has to center on poetry's potential to give man back his reason and understanding, to bring vital force to the values needed in struggling with those dangers. Words for Rielo represent permanent values, specific and definite conquests of the human spirit; their impact is not limited to a small elite, but can touch everyone. He thus uses words to challenge the *idees fixes* of modernity and to revive and re-articulate ancient sacred ideas issuing from Higher Mind. These latter ideas are embodied in his verse, revealing the constituent elements of human nature and specifically the potentiating force or "seed" in man for self-development, higher consciousness and soul. The idea of individual free will and the concept of liberty are underlying motifs in Rielo's lyrics. Are these aspects of man integral elements of human nature? Or is it rather our conditioning and education, our political and economic structures, that are in control,

---

1. The word esoteric comes from the Greek: esoterikos [ἐσωτερικός] : esoteros [ἐσώτερος] meaning inner of eso [ἔσω], within; es, eis, into) 1. a) intended for or understood by only a chosen few, as an inner group of disciples or initiates (said of ideas, doctrines, literature, etc.) b) beyond the undestanding or knowledge of (Webster). In the context of the present study this strict understanding of the word is intended, specifically the "inner meaning" or esoteric meaning. The use of esoteric in any of the sense that it is sometimes understood in countries where Romance languages are spoken as occult, exotic or connected with witchcraft is never intended.

and we mere automatons without free will and real liberty? Rielo bases his answer to these questions on the figure of Christ and especially on Christ's powerful language: sleep, deafness, and blindness are the metaphors through which Christ's parables refer to the mechanical state of being and mechanical consciousness of ordinary, undeveloped man.

Through his mystical poetics, Rielo maintains that without struggle there is no progress or change, that for mechanized, internally undeveloped man no change can come about without a breaking of habits and received ideas. The first duty of language in catalyzing such change is to come to grips with everyday experience. For in order to communicate higher ideas to common man one must take as one's poetic and mystic inspriration all the fundamental elements and experiences of life, since these are the source from which all human aspirations evolve. In the poem quoted at the beginning of this chapter, Rielo returns to the fundamental level of everyday life both through his physically immediate language and by making New York City the symbol for contemporary human experience, be it conscious or unconscious. Mystical poetics casts "light" [luz] on bread, as it were, giving birth [dando luz] to a recognition of the dignity which is an inalienable endowment of those who eat that bread. Thus theirs is more than the simple nourishment of their bodies; they are granted a glimpse of truth through the symbolic communion of which they partake. This communion, far from doing away with one's own personality, makes one aware of its ineluctable singularity. Each person accepts the symbols subjectively in his own way, and the same words awaken in each different responses and impulses.

If we observe, we see to what extent man is insensible to logical reason even though logic appears to play a commanding role in currently dominant modes of thought. What is the cause of this paradoxical condition? Logic has marginalized the other centers in man that also "think": emotions, feelings, instincts, and the body--the affective aspects of man that are in touch with the obscure energies of the world. These energies, however, can be re-awakened by clothing ideas in symbol and metaphor and thus eliciting a response in those whom the naked idea leaves untouched and cold. *Dichtung*, poetic language, has therefore a virtue (in the Heideggerian sense) that we do not remember how to exploit because we cease to recognize that such language flows from the source or heart of natural human needs, that it takes as its task the close examination of the universal desires of men.

We live in a mass-oriented world in which mechanical habits predominate over real instincts; those instincts, suffering from the inability to express themselves, actively seek words or images through which to do so. Even the body's hunger has its dignity, its worthiness for poetic articulation, because to desire bread and light is to desire communion with men who can satisfy this hunger. Rielo reminds his readers of Christ's saying that man does not live by bread alone, but by the light of the spirit. (Mt 4:4)

Fernando Rielo Pardal communes and communicates with the common man through lyrics based on personal, real experience, in recognition of the esoteric truth that any individual *is* the world, and the world *is* him. The philosophic term that Rielo uses to describe this idea is "the infused supernatural." Rielo's lyrics posit the self as world and the world as self, thus corresponding closely to the philosophy of another contemporary spiritual leader and author, J. Krishnamurti. Both of these thinkers speak of an imageless or direct perception in which thought's judging, analyzing, and categorizing operations cease, or are quieted. In esoteric symbol the passive "do" of an ascending octave is struck. "The soul does not think about what she sees./ She sees it... quiet, absorbed, still," (Rielo. *Llanto azul* 62)

Rielo's sees the poet's mission as that of giving word and revealed meaning to the interpenetration of self and world and to the process of direct perception. In examining this notion of the aims of poetry it is important to recall the example of Spanish poetry written during the time of the Civil War and during the post-war period, a body of work which might be called "occupation" poetry. During those years, any poet who ventured to shed light on the dominant logic of appearances came under censorship and risked death or prison. Disruptive or challenging ideas were forbidden. But although the authorized ideology maintained its logic of appearances for close to four decades, it never managed to suppress completely the competing logic of the heart. Before the war a small number of elitist poets had written in rarified verse for the initiated few; but suddenly, under the pressure of oppressive conditions, they began to write and speak at the level of ordinary human sensibilities. This shift indicated not a discontinuity in expression but rather an expansion of poetry's communicative possibilities through an incorporation of the voice of the common man. The words of the poet turned to the ordinary needs, real problems, and virtues of man. Poetic imagery attached itself by the roots to mankind's wounded sensibilities. Language which had been closed to poets before took on new meaning; cold reason could no longer be heard above cries of pain. Symbols, rather than logical thought, provided the fitting language for a situation in which to speak of liberty or the lack of it was to speak from real personal experience rather than from remote intellectual theory.

When this period of post-war oppression ended poetry once again became dispassionate; writers no longer felt the universal longing that made them "greater than themselves." The old mechanical social forms were restored and man's imagination ceased to create anything new. In 1990, however, we find that something closely akin to the *angst* of the post-war period has returned. Our world is in crisis at every level, political, economic and ecological. Indeed, the ecological crisis is of staggering proportions. The rain forests, for example, are disappearing at a rate of thousands and thousands of acres per minute. Their total destruction is calculated to fall in the year 2050 if the process continues unabated. The toxification of the food chain and the water sources is now at near-critical levels and daily increasing. Wars are being fought in almost every part of the world. Moreover, thousands of nuclear weapons are in place for war, enough weapons to destroy all the cities of the northern hemisphere. If a nuclear war takes place, even the few people that survive in countries not directly involved will experience freezing temperatures resulting from the blocking of the sun by the huge smoke clouds produced by the intense firestorms of burning cities, forests, and gas, chemical, and oil reserves. As a consequence of the freezing temperatures, people will face starvation on a scale that dwarfs that which currently afflicts the drought-stricken areas of Africa. A burning question arises from this situation: can we reverse this momentum toward total destruction of our species? Can man awaken from his hypnotic sleep before it is too late?

Rielo's message is that the only starting point for change in our world in crisis is *within individual man*. Individually, each man must free himself from his own personal, internal, invisible world of conflict, competition, anger, envy, violence, pride and hatred. He must recognize with true commitment that he is part of the world and that the world is part of him, that the outer world is but a reflection of our inner world.

Rielo and other contemporary poets in Spain and elsewhere seek to awaken this recognition by taking on the role of the "mystic" in quest of "union with God." That quest involves the struggle for higher development of the internal world, higher states of consciousness and being, that esoteric Christianity calls psycho-transformism. The quest is motivated not by simple self-love, but by a conscious love that recognizes levels of scale and being: the ray of creation beginning in God and proceeding through the sun, the moon, the earth, and man as a living idea-symbol of incomprehensible Higher Mind. Rielo and these poets are new age mystics in that their language and style reflect the mystic power of common man. They are truly revolutionary in their call for complete *metanoia* (μετάνοια), which correctly translated from the Greek means "change of mind." Their call is for reversal, for the turning of reality right-side-up. Their teaching hangs, as it were, in a chrysalis, waiting impatiently to be born, waiting for the power of imagination to crack the imprisoning shell by means of a creative use of language.

Rielo believes that what Western man lacks in his struggle for self-renewal is a *raison d'être*, a motive. Madame de Stael said that nothing in man can become great without the sentiment of the incompleteness of his destiny. This sentiment of one's incompleteness or nothingness for Rielo and other mystics initiates "becoming"; it is the mandatory starting point for raising one's level of being and consciousness. In contemporary society, however, doors are often closed to this kind of change. The scientific, technological revolution has created artificial needs that function to the detriment of the soul, of the development of higher states in oneself. Continual expansion of industry worsens environmental conditions and needs more and more capital and power, so that individually, our reasons for what we do, indeed the basic patterns of lives, are determined primarily by the pressure of money. The lyrical power of an individual with passionate belief in his own accomplishments is lost. Rielo states in a moving poem called "Evocación" ["Evocation"]:

> [... ... ... No, I no longer know
> if I am sob of a mirror or rain
> that the aching body of the asphalt vomits out
> for new greens that will redeem it.]

> ... ... No. Ya no sé
> si soy llanto de un espejo o lluvia
> que el doliente cuerpo del asfalto vomita
> para verdes nuevos que lo rediman.
> (Llanto azul 66)

The situation is somewhat different for the "opponents" of the Western world. From their vantage point as "have-nots" they expect to achieve in a few years what took us much longer to achieve. Their effort is totalitarian. However, even materialism sprung from such revolutionary exhilaration, the exhilaration of overcoming great barriers, carries lyric power. All pure lyric power, however, derives from truly spiritual, rather than material, movements.

Rielo maintains that unless a spiritual "structure" can be restored to language, in part through the efforts of poets, man will ultimately be devoured by the very machines in economics and politics that he created to improve his material life. This is Rielo's answer to the question of how poetry, the act of creating, should present itself in the situation of the contemporary social world. Rielo and other contemporary writers believe that there is still time for the creative spirit to dominate that situation, given sufficient spiritual force and enough powerful individuals behind the effort. It is clear that those who defend only material wealth will inevitably fail. This pursuit invokes fear of loss and is not in harmony with the creative mandate of faith.

Rielo calls his poetry mystic. He envisions the mission of mystic poetry as the restoration of man's ability to believe in himself and the community to which he belongs through union with God. He presents today the opportunity of taking a spiritual risk, a risk from which an unequalled grandeur may result. Although the immense fresco of history unfolds around us and although may we feel like actors simply repeating pre-scripted lines in a universal drama, we *can* be equal to the challenge. The positive note of faith issuing from the spiritual risk is the balanced gaiety of which Yeats speaks:

> All perform their tragic play,
> There struts Hamlet, there is Lear
> That's Ophelia, that Cordelia;
> Yet, they, should the last scene be there,
> The great stage curtain about to drop,
> If worthy their prominent part in the play,
> Do not break up their lines to weep.
> They know that Hamlet and Lear are gay;
> Gaiety transfiguring all that dread.
> All things fall and are built again,
> And those who build them again are gay.   (338-9)

In an untitled poem from *Dolor entre cristales* Rielo himself appears as one of the characters in the drama of life, but with a certain liberty not granted to Hamlet or Lear. The drama is not prewritten. A personal tragedy that would lead most modern men to utter despair is reversed by the power of faith in the world of the spirit represented by Christ. Man ascends; he breaks the chains of the prisoner of destiny:

[I visit the hospital every morning
to remake myself with a leg that's not mine
and to rehabilitate too my broken arm.
I see you beside the sea, my forever friend,
perhaps for its color or its waves
perhaps because the sky that you don't reach
is the clothing that conceals my nakedness.

Your light, oh sea, from sky reflected
is not the light that my breast has hidden:
man is a sob that licks the earth
as you do with your color; that is why
you will never navigate over yourself.

The sick are moving in their wheelchairs
that, ships of pain,
see in the water your indifferent blue.

The hands that cross the corridors,
throbbing with a sadness that smiles,
go looking for their exiled happiness
although their flesh is paining them.
They are so much more than your bluish sea
because man will see Christ one day
walking upon his victorious sob.

Your wheelchair will be Elijah's chariot
which traverses the firmament,
the exercise of pain now forgotten.

If we, invalids, wheel along
with trembling body on the shadowed earth,
Christ dragged His body between the stones
so that in perspective with death

man may one day ascend over a sea
and an earth now forgotten in their nothingness.]

Visito el hospital cada mañana
para hacerme con pierna que no es mía
y habilitar también mi brazo roto.
Te veo junto al mar, mi siempre amigo,
quizás por su color o por sus olas
quizás porque el cielo que no alcanzas
es vestido que encumbre mi desnudo.

Tu luz, oh mar, del cielo reflejada
no es la luz que mi seno tiene oculta:
el hombre es llanto que a la tierra lame
como haces tú con tu color; por eso,
nunca navegarás sobre ti mismo.

Los enfermos se mueven en sus sillas
de ruedas que, navíos del dolor,
ven en su agua tu azul indiferente.

Las manos que recorren los pasillos,
pulsadas de tristeza que sonríe,
van buscando en dicha desterrada
aunque su carne les esté doliendo.
Son mucho más que tu azulado mar
porque el hombre verá a Cristo algún día
caminar en su llanto victorioso.

Vuestra silla de ruedas será carro
de Elías que recorra el firmamemto
ya olvidado el dolor en ejercicio.

Si nosotros, inválidos, rodamos
con cuerpo trémulo en la tierra umbría,
Cristo arrastró su cuerpo entre las piedras
para que en perspectiva con la muerte
el hombre ascienda un día sobre un mar
y una tierra en su nada ya olvidados.   (27-28)

The moving dramatization of the love of God and Christ dominates Rielo's poetry, which situates mankind's hopes and actions in history. The poet suffers life's tragedies and conflicts on the same plane as other men, yet he "speaks" as poet what they need to hear: the deeper truths that he is aware of and can voice via the power of metaphor and symbol. He understands the essential values and holds fast to what is permanent in their transitory forms. Rielo could be called a modern hero saved from contradiction and self-doubt, though, as for all heroes, there is an element of failure in his life, an element depicted in the poem just quoted as well as in others. Showing his humility in the revelation of his personal tragedies, he becomes one among the many who suffer such tragedies. Thus he is the modern hero, the anonymous man in the street who may suffer and die alone in silence for his idea of himself--an idea which is also mysteriously our own. We can feel with him the achievement of any man who does not surrender to the overwhelming fatalism of our era. He is the son [el hijo] who speaks with and is spoken to by God his Father [Padre]. As son and poet, he is the creator by Word of the power of hope, love and faith. He affirms with certainty that man can rise from the dead both in life and after death. The descent into hell or "dark night of the soul" is merely that part of the hero's destiny in which he must experience and overcome the monsters of the self and the monsters of the world. He "returns" strengthened in his belief in the vitality of man, prepared to meet the challenges of the world's absurdity with words and deeds.

The idea of man as illimitable, as carrying the essence of Divinity appears in many cultures and in many eras. Great thinkers of the past have described the spiritual or Divine Nature of the inner structure of the universe. Emerson, for example, speaks of timeless, "transcendental" laws which execute themselves. They are out of time, out of space, and not subject to circumstance:

Thus, in the soul of man there is a justice whose retributions are instant and entire. He who does a good deed is instantly ennobled. He who does a mean deed is by the action itself contracted. He who puts off impurity thereby puts on purity. If a man is at heart just, then in so far is he God; the safety of God, the immortality of God, the majesty of God, do enter into that man with justice.... Character is always known. Thefts never enrich; alms never impoverish; murder will speak out of stone walls. The least admixture of a lie--for example, the taint of vanity, any attempt to make a good impression, a favorable appearance--will instantly vitiate the effect. But speak the truth, and all things alive or brute are vouchers, and the very roots of the grass underground there do seem to stir and move to bear your witness. For all things proceed out of the same spirit, which is differently named love, justice, temperance, in its different applications, just as the ocean receives different names on the several shores which it washes. In so far as he [man] roves from being he shrinks ... he becomes less and less, a mote, a point, until absolute badness is absolute death. The perception of this law awakens in the mind a sentiment which we call the religious sentiment, and which makes our highest happiness. Wonderful is its power to charm and to command. It is a mountain air. It is the embalmer of the world. It makes the sky and the hills sublime, and the silent song of the stars is it. It is the beatitude of man. It makes him illimitable. When he says "I ought"; when love warns him; when he chooses, warned from on high, the good and great deed; then, deep melodies wander through his soul from supreme wisdom. Then he can worship, and be enlarged by his worship; for he can never go behind this sentiment. All the expressions of this sentiment are sacred and permanent in proportion to their purity. [They] affect us more than all other compositions. The sentences of the olden time, which ejaculate this piety, are still fresh and fragrant. And the unique impression of Jesus upon mankind, whose name is not so much written as ploughed into the history of this world, is proof of the subtle virtue of this infusion. (*Miscellanies* 120)

Rielo's verse echoes Emerson's melodic meditation on the fundamentally illimitable nature of man. For Rielo however, the awakening of man to his illimitable nature involves a serious commitment to moral action and to making moral value fundamental to the very language of poetry. A recent poem written in the United States, the country whose destiny Rielo believes will achieve universality in "combining, purifying and filtering the Latin and Anglo-Saxon essences," examplifies this commitment. The absurdity challenged in this poem is racism; the essence of the poem, however, and its mode of expression are mystical:

[Woman of the purest of blackness lying
in a wheelchair
illness incurable
written in her gaze.

The company of her husband
and her daughter were radiating the mysterious enchantment
of a tenderness that no valley can offer
with its voluptuous living greenness.

How overwhelming was the sadness in her rose glance!
Is there anything more suggestive on the earth,
waiting room in which are seated
life, pain and death?
Each and every race carrying their wounds on high.

I kissed her on her wide forehead: brief moment
in which two colors became one
alive, in the ineffable smile of a soul
that escapes from its wounded flesh.

When I had crossed the Manhattan bridge
I understood that also steel
passed through fire cries out.
How much more will a soul cry out whose iron
is an iron more ancient than all the earth?]

Mujer de negritud purísima postrada
en su silla de ruedas
por incurable invalidez
escrita en su mirada.

La compañía de su esposo
y de su hija irradiaban el misterioso encanto
de una ternura que no ofrece el valle
con su verdeante viveza.

¡Cuánta era su tristeza en su mirada rosa!
¿Algo más sugestivo en una tierra,
sala de espera en que se sientan
vida, dolor y muerte?
Todas las razas llevan a cuestas sus heridas.

La besé en su ancha frente: breve instante
en el que dos colores se fundieron,
vivientes, en sonrisa inefable de un alma
que escapa de su carne dolorida.

Cuando hube atravesado el puente de Manhattan
comprendí que también el hierro
pasado por el fuego llora.
¿Cuánto más lo hará un alma que su hierro
es hierro más antiguo que la tierra?
(Dolor entre cristales 40)

In this poem, Rielo does not analyze racism. He does not pretend
to advise as to what "should be" or "could be." Rather, he presents the
kiss on the forehead as the mystic touch that compassion elevates to a
world of radical change where conflict has ceased and where God's
love *is*. The experience is the imaging of feelings and experiences
beyond thought or analysis, of the unitive seeing of total awareness that
ends conflict and ends racism. All negatives are absorbed, dissolved
in this new world of higher consciousness. This unitive seeing is an
action of a new order. It transcends conflict because it reveals all things
as involved with living energy. The total awareness it generates
ultimately results in freedom from misery and suffering, violence and
hatred. It initiates a new state of being, a radical inward change in one's
perception of reality that can end hatred and racism. Only this inward,
individual change can one day result in outward changes in society.

One of the most important elements of poetry--an element often
overlooked by critics--is the experience of joy it gives to its readers.
This joy constitutes a form of higher communication because it affects
the most problematical area for man in his efforts to raise his level of
consciousness: negative emotions. The negative elements of the
emotional center rule the lives of most men and must be made passive
in order to activate such emotions as love, hope, and faith. Rielo's verse
turns sharply from the negative emotions that rule mankind through its
"Yes branches," "Yes trees," "Yes birds,"--a whole world of "Yes," of
positive emotion. His mystic voice affirms the reality of the "Kingdom
of Heaven," a space in present time and in this world where man is not
asleep, not hypnotized by the negativity of life--a space in which men
and women can develop their true essence or real "I," behind which
stands God.

Like Martin Heidegger (who, although an atheist, studied
theology and laid the philosophical foundations for such theologians
as Paul Tillich), Rielo maintains that the question of Being is the central
problem of philosophy. Man, as Heidegger maintains in *Being and*

32

Time, is always in a world he did not make and did not choose. Only man has the capacity to comprehend the past and thus to use it to shape and influence his own destiny. Language, for Heidegger, constitutes man's principal means of achieving such comprehension, especially as used by poets, whom he envisioned as seekers of truth and the essence of being. Rielo initiates in his philosophy a similar reflection on the ultimate nature of Being and reality as manifested in man's filial relationship to his creator, the relationship through which man is enabled to understand and transform the world into which he is born. His philosophy amounts to a theory of poetic living, of a way of life aesthetically open to every kiss, every bird, every tree, every race.

Rielo has broken fresh ground. He has the courage to go forward to create his own poetic world of the spirit without asking if he is following others or if they are following him or even if he is understood. His faith in his own reality requires no such confirmation. His poetic union with the spirit, with God is tender and intense self-surrender without self-destruction. His heart is pure and his intelligence loving, as he moves through the universe he knows: leaves, cities, birds, kiss. His is mysticism of a new and modern order.

II

Distinctions Between
Religious And Mystic Poetry

Many Spanish poets of the twentieth century have underscored the need for a consciousness of man's link to transcendental realities, and have therefore committed the poetic word to a search for spiritual support. These poets seek eternal truth and a reality that extends beyond earthbound limits. Their search is motivated, however, by a shared sense of being dispossessed of God--of being distanced from God and alien to His intimacy, no matter how comfortable the poet feels within the spiritual coordinates which God's existence furnishes him. This search has been undertaken, with varying degrees of intensity, in the works of such writers as Miguel de Unamuno, Antonio Machado, Juan Ramón Jiménez, Dámaso Alonso, Luis Cernuda, Luis Felipe Vivanco, José María Valverde, Germán Bleiberg, Gabriel Celaya, Blas de Otero, and others.

It goes without saying that such a wide configuration of poets can hardly be represented as a homogenous bloc. Leaving aside differences in generation and style, these poets can be divided (albeit not always in a clearly dichotomized fashion) into two groups, which Dámaso Alonso has defined as the "deeply rooted" and the "uprooted" (*Poetas...* 345), depending of the nature of their response to their sense of being dispossessed of or distanced from God. Discontented and nonconformist, the "uprooted" poets would storm their way into heaven with complaints and histrionic threats which border on provocation. The "deeply rooted" poets, however, respond not with anger but with sorrow when they see how far away they are from God's center of vision. For example, in "Las manos ciegas" ["Blind Hands"] Leopoldo Panero laments the absence of God:

[My entire heart, glowing human ember,
useless without Thy love, empty without Thee,
searches for Thee in the night,
I feel it searching, like a blind man
when he walks he stretches out his hands so full
of wideness and of joy.]

Todo mi corazón, ascua de hombre,
inútil sin tu amor, sin Tí vacío,
en la noche te busca,
le siento que te busca, como un ciego
que extiende al caminar las manos llenas
de anchura y de alegría   (165)

Another "deeply rooted" poet, Carlos Busoño, though counting on
a faith sufficient to prevent his view of the world from undergoing a
radical crisis, nonetheless experiences an inner shudder when he
recognizes the unrelenting transience to which all things are subject:

[Let us save it all,
there's not much time, this area.
save the jalopy and the mattress and the old car-cover,
the fireplace coals, the firepoke, the hat.]

Salvémoslo todo,
queda poco tiempo, este campo.
salvemos el carromato, el colchón, la vieja cubierta del coche
el carbón del hogar, el atizador, el sombrero.
                    ("Salvación de la Vida" ["Saving of Life"] *Invasión* 192)

The panorama of twentieth-century Spanish religious poetry is
dominated by the work of Fernando Rielo, whose verse is religious in
the deepest sense--in its interpretation of the inner meanings of
religion and Christianity. Rielo's poetry is described by literary critics,
scholars and journalists not only as religious, however, but also as
mystic, and Rielo, himself a learned scholar of Spanish literature, a
theologian, and a priest, agrees with this categorization of his poetry.
Thus, in order fully to comprehend Rielo's poetic achievement, one
needs to draw a firm distinction between broadly religious poetry and
specifically mystical poetry, a distinction which must in turn be based

on a clear definition of the concept of mysticism both in general and as it has manifested itself in the Spanish poetic tradition.

The word *mystic* comes from the Greek *mystikos*, [μυστικός] meaning secret; it signifies by inference something hidden or not known to the masses, not obvious. From this root are derived the various contemporary meanings of the term *mysticism* listed in *Webster:* first, the doctrine of an immediate spiritual intuition of truths believed to transcend ordinary understanding, or of a direct, intimate union of the soul with the divinity through love; second, "spiritually significant or symbolic," pertaining to mysteries known only to initiates; third, a power or significance of obscure or mysterious character. Thus we see mystics defined as those who attain insight into the mysteries transcending ordinary human knowledge as by immediate intuition in a state of spiritual ecstasy. Through empirical cognition, they seek to know a Higher Mind or Higher Power, transcending the limits of the individual self. Thus mysticism's notions of knowledge and being directly oppose those of solipsism, in which the self is the only object of verifiable knowledge and in which nothing but the self is posited as existing. Finally, it should be noted that knowledge of an esoteric or hidden nature is often passed down through oral tradition by word of mouth from teacher to disciple. As Ouspensky points out in *In Search of the Miraculous*, "hidden knowledge" and mystical states of consciousness have almost always been closely linked. Ouspensky explains mysticism as a breaking through of hidden knowledge into our consciousness.

In his *Historia de la literatura española*, Angel del Río offers an account of the most important features specific to the Spanish mystical tradition, noting especially those elements in that tradition that are drawn from the works of Plato and Plotinus:

1. Desire for God and the awakening of the soul when it senses God. Conversion.

2. Purification or the purgative way. Penitence, discipline, detachment from things of the senses in order to reach a state of grace.

3. Illuminative way, contemplation, meditation, concentration of the soul --will of the intellect and the feeling-- in God.

36

4.Dark night of the soul; and

5.Unitive way: marriage, spiritual union with God. (256)

In his excellent study *La poesía mística de Fernando Rielo* (1985), Aldo R. Forés states that Rielo's poetry represents a rebirth of Spanish mystical poetry. Forés defines mystical poetry as poetry that speaks of God, of God in intimate union with the soul, of God in all that is (pg.10). Forés' definition draws on the work of Helmut Hatzfeld, who, in *Estudios literarios sobre la mística española*, speaks of the double function of the mystic poet: first, to apprehend God, and, second, to submit himself to the process of transporting this apprehension to a work of art, to mystic poetry (11). Authentic and genuine mystic poetry expresses the mystical phenomena, the mystical experience, the union of the soul with its creator. Hatzfeld underscores the role of truly symbolic and poetic language in revealing the direct experience of God.

Renowned poet, novelist, and critic Odón Betanzos Palacios, president of the North American *Real Academia Española de la Lengua*, agrees with Dr. Forés in his classification of Rielo's poetry as mystical. In the introduction of one of Rielo's collections of verse, *Balcón a la bahía* [Balcony on the Bay], Betanzos states:

[...If there are surrealistic elements in the poetry of Rielo, elements restrained, or rather, overcome by the existential, the mystical nonetheless prevails and defines his poetry, and this happens not so much through the understanding generated by words as through inclination, immersion, aspiration and flight.

I believe, I acknowledge that we are face to face with a book of mystic truth. It is sincere in surrender of the soul, and symbolic in the message of the soul that it offers. It is poetically clean, becoming more clean and loving in the intention that conducts it. I believe, I acknowledge also, that the contemporary mysticism of Rielo ties in well with the mystical manners and wills of our past mystics]. (8-9)

Betanzos' comments on the mystical character of Rielo's work are echoed by those of David Murray in the prologue to *Llanto azul* [Blue Sob]. Murray informs readers that Rielo's poetry is within the framework of mystical poetry and that it represents a renewal of the mystical tradition of Spanish literature, which found its supreme expression in Spanish Golden Age mystics such as San Juan de la Cruz and Santa Teresa (5). A wide range of Spanish and Latin American press reviewers of *Llanto azul* reached the same conclusion. In *Nueva Andalucia* (Seville), for example, Francisco Anglada writes:

[*Llanto azul*] is like a fascinating renascence of mystical poetry dressed in a new style and very much linked to the demands of a new Christian humanism.]

And in *El Pueblo* (Arequipa, Perú), Adolfo Venegas writes:

[It is well-known that Fernando Rielo exhibits clear inferences from Solomon's "Song of Songs" and the mystical poetry of St. John of the Cross, although the influence of the Gospels is even more pronounced in an internalized manner. Suffice it to say that *Llanto azul* is a book infused with a living, working faith whose word becomes shaped into an entirely original state of mysticism.]

Finally, one should note that this recognition of the mystical nature of Rielo's poetry is also confirmed by his fellow-poets. In a short speech introducing Fernando Rielo's works to the *Agrupación Literaria Amigos de la Poesía* [Friends of Poetry Literary Group], for exmaple, the Spanish Valencian poet Alama Martí stated:

[In Fernando Rielo we meet contemporary Spanish mysticism, equally deep, equally profound, and equally as graceful as the poetic mysticism which the Spanish saints elevated to the symbolic level...]

And in a 1979 letter to the *Idente* school (the international educational institution founded by Rielo), Dámaso Alonso makes a comparison between his own poetry and Rielo's that both confirms Martí's point and forges a crucial distinction between religious and mystical poetry:

[My own poetry is not really mystical, but merely religious. It abounds in contradictions between deism and atheism, although the former clearly predominates.... It differs roundly from that of Rielo, which is always delicate and smooth, whereas my own (in *Hijos de la ira*, [Children of Fury] is almost always rough, sometimes even brutal.] (Letter)

Apparently, Alonso has never elaborated upon the distinction between religious and mystical poetry that he formulates in this passage. But since, I believe, this distinction is fundamental to any full understanding of Rielo's work, I will pursue it further, examining four major criteria by which these kinds of poetry may be differentiated. First, one must note that the mystical poet's union with the divine contrasts sharply with the state of deprived dispossession characteristic of religious poets, be they "deeply rooted" or "uprooted." The point of departure is God Himself. The mystic poet does not feel displaced by Him, nor mistreated by His divine hand. One must not confuse the religious poet's laments with those expressions of purifying atonement or penitence which del Rio defines as a fundamental element of mystical poetry and through which the mystical poet gains access to the "illuminative way" that leads to the state of oneness with God.

Another way to formulate this contrast is to note that while the religious poet assumes that an unbridgeable gap separates him from God, the mystical poet places his faith in a radical inward transformation that enables him to achieve the state of oneness with God. The mystic is thus a revolutionary in the psychological sense. He calls for an awakening to the only "way", the only "truth," the only "life" through which humanity can rein in its self-destructive energies. This awakening must occur, through the contemplative awareness to which poetry is one means of invoking, in the inner space of the self, in one's thoughts, feelings, and imagination. Suddenly, instantaneously, one sees the truth for the very first time, through direct revelation rather than through analytic thinking. Hence, even the symbolic language of the mystic is revelatory rather than descriptive, definitive, or denotative, for it bears the burden of a message that cannot be reached through the workings of reason, a message which can only be comprehended through the experience of transformation.

That message itself constitutes a second criterion by which mystical and religious poetry may be differentiated. The themes of religious poetry are often primarily personal: personal longing for God, personal thoughts about spiritual aspects of life, ideas of life after death, etc. Such poetry, though it may offer occasional intuitions of a higher reality, remains caught the world of desire for things of this life and for things of the unawakened self. The message borne by the mystic, by contrast, centers on the notion of "man asleep," of the need for man to be awakened through a development of the interior world

39

of consciousness and being. Seeing man as God's experiment in self-development, the mystic teaches that man must free himself of the desire for things of the unawakened self, that man must strive, through a radical and inward change of being, to enter into God's field of vision. In a poem called *¡Qué daría!* from *Dios y árbol*, Rielo writes:

[What would I not give, my God, that you might want
me to love you like no one ever has!

Do you have perhaps so strong a hand
as to make it so...?

Ah, if only I could...
now I have told you.

That in my passion I might die
and You... might see me, see me.]

¡Qué daría, Dios mío, porque Tú quisieras
que yo te amara como nadie hizo!

¿Tienes acaso mano tan fuerte
que lo haga posible...?

Ay, si yo pudiera...
ya te lo he dicho.

Que en mi deseo muera
y Tú... me veas, me veas.   (90)

Perhaps the most distinctive--and most distinctively mystical--feature of Rielo's poetry is an essential freedom of mind, a freedom not limited by yesterday's experience or tomorrow's hope, a freedom made possible by the dying out of this-worldly desire. His poetry is thus alive in the present moment, spontaneous and vivifying. Through it, the reader enters into the contemplative state of mind where truth can come into being, and where God is directly perceived in a state of mystic ecstasy.

Rielo's handling of the poetic message can be summed up by referring to St. Bonaventure's dictum that the poet or orator must express "what is in him"--meaning not that the poet must express his inner subjective realm, but rather that he must give expression to an idea that he has made so thoroughly his own that its expression takes some decisively original form. Through the mode of expression St. Bonaventure prescribes, form and content become a unity. Such a poetic art both imitates and expresses the themes by which it is informed; the idea, as it were, is made flesh. And if that idea is a truly mystical one, its materialization in poetic form opens the possibility for a fundamental transformation of the reader's or listener's understanding and being. Rielo's mysticism is therefore neo-platonic in the sense that "the reason why a given object is beautiful is that it has a gorgeous colour of shape or any other such attribute, I disregard all these other explanations - I find them all confusing - and I cling simply and straightforwardly and no doubt foolishly to the explanation that the one thing that makes that object beautiful is the presence in it or association with it (in whatever way the relation comes about) of absolute Beauty." (Plato, "Phaedo" 159)

A third characteristic that distinguishes mystical from religious poetry is the former's infused meditative element. Many of Rielo's poems seem to be an invitation to contemplation, a contemplation in which the mind is quieted, a contemplation in which the rolling, mechanical thoughts triggered by every passing turn of external events are stilled. In this non-thinking state of meditative reflection, a true listening to and understanding of the messages of one's own inward higher centers becomes possible. In her essay "The Mystical Meditative Content of Fernando Rielo's *Llanto azul*," Edna Simms confirms this point when she defines the contemplative element of Rielo's poetry as the source of its transformative power:

> Fernando Rielo evokes the mystical moment by inviting the reader to contemplate the most impressive facets of nature. In "Sierra," he gives movement to a great immobile mass where "leonine wraths" appear changed into a "sweet smile" after being touched by "angelic crystals." The breeze of this "beloved rock" with its "perfumed breath" is presented as powerful enough to provoke the memory of man's most sublime moment. When the soul is united to God, man for the first time feels the perfect state which the Father of the world had in mind from the first instant He conceived the idea of forming His creation. (13)

And in a poem titled "*Alzate*" ["Rise Up"] Rielo himself affirms the importance of contemplation and meditation by making silence the link between the world of nature and God:

[Your breeze is a pilgrim trill in tones
that colors pour like faces of dawn
in smooth rivers that laugh in the valley.
They laugh and sing virgin groves
that disrobe the waters of their open brilliance
and the fish watch and promptly drink.
Is it not perhaps the sweet trill extensive valley
that quickly upon the lip its silence merges?

Oh silence...

Thin lip shining in the night.
No. No. The slender moon tells us nothing now.
even the sun... hardly lights up
the rustic fields of a weeping soul,
the mountain, the deer and the birds...
hide in their sob that which lives eternal:

You, Father.]

Tu brisa es de un trino peregrino en tonos
que colores vierte como rostros de aurora
en los tersos ríos que en el valle ríen.
Ríen y cantan vírgenes florestas
que desnudan aguas de sus cándidos brillos
y los peces miran y presurosos beben.
¿no es acaso el dulce trino extenso valle
que presto al labio su silencio infunde?

Oh silencio...

Fino labio que en la noche brilla.
No. No. La esbelta luna ya nada nos dice.
Hasta el sol... apenas enciende
los campos agrestes de un alma que llora.

El monte, el corzo y el ave...
en su llanto esconden lo que eterno subsiste:

Tú, Padre.

(Llanto azul 103)

Silent, meditative tranquility brings a state in which the reality of God can be perceived. The state of tranquility is a creative state in that the external conditionings of the world, whether political or religious, are left behind. There is a new freedom in this creative state. The "silent" mind is not a trained mind but one that understands the limits of thinking and the new possibilities of knowing and feeling that lie beyond it: an intelligent *awareness*.

A fourth and final distinction between religious and mystical poetry can be traced in the contrast between their respective exoteric and esoteric approaches to and expressions of spiritual teachings. Rielo's work clearly exemplifies entering into the esoteric, hidden meaning of a spiritual theme like the Trinity--the Father, the Son, and the Holy Ghost. In his verse and philosophy, the Trinity symbolizes the three forces which are present in all manifestations of reality. First Force is the active Force, symbolically the "Father" in Rielo's poetry, while the Second Force, symbolized by Rielo as the "Son," is the resisting force, always also present in the very nature of things. The true Third Force or "Holy Ghost," however, is not present in ordinary man before development. The things of this-worldly life--that is, personal ambitions and desires--are the ordinary man's Third Force. A change of being can occur only when this ordinary Third Force "dies" (or is made passive) and is replaced by the Third Force from a higher level. This higher Third Force is the wisdom and the knowledge that will produce for those who bring it to bear a new life--the growth or development of that part of oneself that originated from above. Personality, which has been developed in this-worldly life and which can function only as a machine programmed to react to external circumstance, gradually becomes passive and essense the "spark of the divine flame" burns higher. Through this process, a process that involves both effort and suffering, one gains the potential to act, to determine one's own life, to escape to some degree the law of accident and come under what Rielo calls the law of destiny.

To clarify further the distinction presented in this chapter between religious and mystical poetry, it will be helpful to explore the

43

philosophical model of Genetic Metaphysics through which Rielo elaborates systematically his concept of the three forces as immanent in all manifestations of reality. The relation between these forces, Rielo maintains, is at once metaphysical and filial. The conflict between active First Force and resistant Second Force initiates a transformation, albeit often partial or incomplete, of ordinary experience into higher Third Force, a transformation through which a synthesis of First and Second forces is achieved and the conflict between them is, on one level, at least, resolved. This synthesis produces something new, a heightened level of being or "being +." Insofar as the transformation that engenders this "being +" remains incomplete, however, insofar as the higher Third Force still remains mixed with lower concerns and desires, the necessity remains for "being +" to in turn become the First and Second Forces for a new manifestation in which the transformative process may be re-enacted on a yet higher level. In Rielo's metaphysics, this dynamic governs man's inner world, the world of earthly nature, and the higher world of the planets and stars. Its originating force is God, Who takes on three aspects--God the Father, God the Son, and God the Holy Ghost--the third constituting the locus in which these three forces become One. Their emanation into the world of matter separates. The expansion of consciousness in man is brought about by uniting them again.

In his essay "La metafísica pura en Fernando Rielo," the noted Spanish theologian and philosopher José M. López Sevillano, argues that Rielo's Genetic Metaphysics belongs to a postmodern phase in the history of philosophy. Lopez points out that Rielo's unprecedented model of metaphysics purifies Christian thought: although it surveys both metaphysical and phenomenological fields of investigation, it ultimately moves beyond the phenomenological field to take up ontological questions, to become a transcendental science of being. Through this transcendentalizing move, Rielo's Genetic Metaphysics provides a means of comprehending what is fundamental or essential to human consciousness, that essential core of which López writes:

> ...this is the reason for the universality of creeds and states of beliefs that endeavor to interpret the most profound sense of the human being: his nature, his origin and his destiny. (1)

The key to Rielo's purified Genetic Metaphysics is the opposition between the concept "flowed from, or emanated," on one hand, and the concept "created, made, or begotten," on the other--an opposition also fundamental to the overall distinction between mystical and religious poetry. Rielo sees the subject-object relation not as one in which a subject creates or begets an object which then assumes a fully separate existence, but rather as one in which the object flows or emanates from the subject and thus remains part of it by "congenesis". As López states:

> The two beings $S_1 \doteq^1 S_2$ constitute, at the same time, sole genetic conception of the substance [congenesis], sole genetic conception of the essence [transverberation], sole genetic conception of existence [circumgenesis], sole genetic conception of nature [conformgenesis], sole genetic conception of the processions [circumlogesis]....

The geneticity of the principle of relation consists in that S_1 is the *gene*[2] of S_2. The agent [S_1] defines, therefore, with generative definition, theoretical generation, its object [S_2]. S_2 does not receive, for its part, existence from S_1, given that it already has it with the same constitutive exigency as S_1 in virtue of constituting, in genetic complementarily, sole absolute subject and principle. The genetic model renders impossible, by the same genetic nature of its terms [$S_1 \doteq S_2$], absolute monism and dualism.[3] (7)

The S_1 in Rielo's philosophical model is not universal life but an emanation of universal life, its essence being pure spirit, or infinite, eternal mind. S_2, man's spirit, is the soul of his soul which is immortal by nature of its "congenesis", its oneness with the Father. Together with intentional asetic strivings and conscious work for being, this concept of S_2 as flowing or emanating from S_1, this concept of congenesis, separates Rielo's poetry decisively from merely religious poetry. The mystic understands that God, while living apart in His essence, is still within this universe and this universe is within Him. S_1 genetizes S_2; S_2 is genetized by S_1. The symbol of complementarity in Rielo's philosophical model is the "equal" sign [$\doteq$] as it appears between two metaphysical extremes like the origin and replica and establishes between them not only a transitive relation of subject to object but a congenerative, copular relation of subject to complement. The intense

---

1. $\doteq$ Means intrinsic logical complementarity between two terms.

2.   Pronounced [xene].

3.   López refers in this statement to Rielo's presentation titled "Genetic Conception of the Principle of Relation," which was given at the III World Congress of Christian Philosophy in Quito, Ecuador in 1989.

lyricism and heightened emotional quality of mystical poetry issues from the congenerative vision of the *unumsumus* of God as an active, suffering, rejoicing spirit, a suffering conscious love. An example appears in *Dolor entre cristales*:

[The torrential rains never sway the country;
yes they tremble the long flower stem and converts it into mud.
This is the exact instant for you to walk
with bare and humble foot and your hands toward heaven
looking at the horizon where God appears
and with a single gesture toward him he lifts up your footstep
and, washed by angel, he delivers it over to the divine
smile

... I Know of nothing so far, far.]

Las lluvias torrenciales nunca mecen el campo;
sí estremecen la espiga y en lodo la convierten.
Este es exacto instante para que tú camines
con descalzo pie humilde y tus manos al cielo
mirando el horizonte por si Dios aparece
para con sólo un gesto hacia sí el paso te alce,
y, lavado por ángel, lo entregue a la divina
sonrisa

... No conozco nada más lejos, lejos.   (95)

The notion of unity fundamental to congenesis is also manifested in the *unitive seeing* of the mystic. Normal mind is conditioned to the process of analysis. We continually separate the observer from the observed, the observer remaining caught within a world of past memories and thus unable to enter fully into the experience of the present. The unitive seeing found in Rielo's work and in other mystical texts refuses rigid distinctions observer and observed or present and past. The observer and the observed unite but objectively, impartially, simultaneously. Thus mysticism is poetry of the active present. It is poetry of action, not in the past or the future but in the present moment--the eternal now that touches eternity at right angles from this position. It is not a poetry of analysis or, like most religious verse, a

poetry of unfulfilled longings or future dreams. As the last poem of
the volume *Dolor entre cristales* puts it:

[How many millions of men
with multitude of centuries in their bones
existed before you, Christ, were born.
Oh Christ, how modern you are!

Love, Love! So slow are you
in unpaining the pain of this life
or sunset so swift that time
you hold back in order
to be something more than something:
perhaps so that time might see
with undone sob.

This is the oldest love!
The most ancient of fires
that has burned up the endless desire
of an illusion that is born and at the same time dies.

Eternal love how much does it cost you
to harvest man!

This is his complaint because he judges you omnipotent.]

Cuántos millones de hombres
con multitud de siglos en sus huesos
fueron antes que Tú, Cristo, nacieras.
¡Oh Cristo, qué moderno eres!

¡Amor, amor! Tan lento eres
en desdoler el dolor de esta vida
o acaso tan veloz que al tiempo
retienes para ser algo más que algo:
quizás para que el tiempo mire
con llanto destrozado.

¡Este es amor tan viejo!
El más anciano de los fuegos
que ha quemado el anhelo interminable
de un ensueño que nace y al mismo tiempo muere.

    ¡Eterno amor, cuánto te cuesta
    recolectar al hombre!

Esta es su queja porque te juzga omnipotente. (105)

Here the fire of the "love so old" burns "the endless desire / of an illusion that is born and at the same time dies," that is, the illusory longings and dreams that ordinarily distract one from present experience. This poem draws on the tradition of the classic mystic love encounter, and though the voice shifts the object of its address from Christ to "love," it does so only to show that eternal love is God's essence.

In all of Rielo's work this love is the force that energizes unitive vision and that enables congenesis. It reflects genetically the possibility of a complete man or woman, a developed "I." In our present state, however, this possibility is rarely realized because we generally fail to practice the first function that we possess as conscious creatures: awareness. It is like the Biblical parable of Leaven in the bread. Awareness is totally different than thinking. One involves physical sensation, impartial observation. The other involves reason or associative thinking. Is this awareness the mystical intangible called soul? Higher consciousness cannot be communicated in ordinary words, which are part of the thought process. Moreover, awareness or the feeling of the whole of myself cannot be summed up as physical action, thought, or feeling. It is a sacred condition that brings one nearer to higher inward centers that know much they are unable to communicate to a mind constantly whirling in egoistic thought.

III

Original And Classical Features
Of Mysticism

Fernando Rielo's relation to the classical mystical tradition is complex: on one hand, he preserves and revives crucial features of that tradition; on the other, he also transforms certain elements of mysticism in new and original ways. In tracing this relation, one must recognize the work of literary critics who have studied Rielo's poetry in the setting of the *Idente* school. These scholars' area of specialization is Spanish mystical poetry and their publications on Rielo deal comparatively and specifically with the mystical aspects of his poetry, particularly his early poetry. The *Idente* school, as I pointed out in the Foreword, is an international educational institution with branches in many countries around the globe, including Europe, South America and the United States. The professors of the school are highly dedicated men and women who devote their activities to the education of young people of many nations. The scope of the education they provide encompasses spiritual and moral values, Spanish language and culture, law, medicine, philosophy, and literature. The *Idente* scholars who have written in depth on the mystic aspects of Rielo include Santiago Acosta, José María López Sevillano, Luis Casasús, A.G. Murray.

One of the most significant results of their research includes an explanation of Rielo's introduction into mystical poetry of the new "genetic" model, as contrasted with the "bridegroom-bride," "husband-wife," or "lover-beloved" models found in the classic Spanish mystics like San Juan de la Cruz and Santa Teresa. The latter's imagery is derived from the *Song of Songs* and seeks to express poetically the consummation of love between Christ and the Christian. Thus we find their works abound in such terms as "spiritual marriage" and "mystical betrothal." Rielo's genetic model, in contrast, focuses on the father-son relationship as the key to mystical consummation or union. This "genetic principle" of filial love is for Rielo more faithful to the message of the New Testament, which is the springboard of his verse and which he often quotes in order to introduce his poetry. The sexual connotations inherent in the traditional mystic imagery are absent in Rielo's model. Rather than becoming "husbands" or "wives," we are "children" of God and Christ. The *Idente* scholars believe that an understanding of this new model of genetic imagery is fundamental for readers who would enter into the complete experience of Rielo's mysticism. A poem that clearly reveals the genetic model is *"Día claro"* [Clear Day]:

[And you, Father, when at last, reached by me
When the tear of my flesh dead
When I shout to you from my firm flight: I have overcome the
world!
When you see me thus, toward You
swift, without spurs, without shirt...
you will tell me then, I am sure, you announced it to me
that simply clear day:

        ---you will enter my bosom,
        from whence you were born.

My bosom is yours!

This is, yes, the end of so many kisses
that we have exchanged. And today... of those
that, lie buried in the tomb
of my lost youth.

I greet you, today with these lines:

        ---Good morning
        Father.]

Y Tú, Padre, cuando, al fin, por mí alcanzado...
Cuando la lágrima de mi carne muerta...
Cuando te grite en mi vuelo firme: ¡vencí al mundo!
Cuando así me veas, hacia Ti...
raudo, sin espuelas y sin camisa...
me dirás entonces, estoy seguro, me lo anunciaste
aquel día simplemente claro:

> ---entrarás en mi seno,
> de donde nacieras.

¡Mi seno es tuyo!

Este es, sí, el fin de tantos besos
que nos hemos dado. Y hoy... de aquellos
que, enterrados yacen en el sepulcro
de mi juventud perdida.

Yo te saludo, hoy, con estos versos:

> ---Buenos días,
> Padre.
> (*Llanto azul* 79)

Another closely related feature of Rielo's poetry explained by the *Idente* scholars is what they call the *Poe'S*, a term originated by Rielo himself. The *Poe'S* is the form or "root" of the poem, the genetic value expressed by means of the lyrical and mystical. Linguistic material is only a consequence of this form or root. As Lopez Sevillano puts it,

Each poem reaches its climax in the *Poe'S*, and the fruitive and contemplative, synthesized in the unitive, herein acquire their fullest meaning. The mystical poem, then, is the result of a transverberation which radiates out from the *Poe'S* and becomes explicit in being projected upon each and every line of poetry; the poem is not, therefore, segmental or composed of juxtapositions of images, metaphors, or signs. By way of comparison, the *Poe'S* is the sap that courses through the poetic entity's veins and manifests itself as the form and defining element of the poem. (López Sevillano, Introduction xv)

Thus the *Poe'S* is the internal dynamic acting as content and as such cannot be analyzed by means of customary formalistic approaches, in which the technical composition of the work is the main object of study. The *Poe'S* is embedded in each and every line of Rielo's verse, transforming each line into what López Sevillano calls a "metapoem," a mode of ordering mystical evocations which enter into the creative act:

> This metapoem is aesthetically prior to all linguistic determinations and serves to unite the semantic, syntactic, and phonetic strata of the resulting text in the light of its poetic genesis. It may thus be affirmed that in Fernando Rielo's poetry the *Poe'S*, as the theoretical and operative synthesis, instead of being subject to linguistic limitations, subjects language to its own dynamic and enables this poetry to be "transplanted" from one cultural soil to another without thereby losing its essential values. (López Sevillano, Introduction xxv).

Through the *Poe'S*, in other words, Rielo's poetry frees itself from literary conventions and makes itself easily translatable as meaning and experience into other languages.

The *Poe'S*, as López Sevillano explains, may be found in the verse by deploying a method of reduction which leads to an implicit or explicit maxim or proverb:

> To determine what the poet intends to communicate, along with his personal conception and poetic, literary, and artistic values, we must begin with the *Poe'S*, not the line of poetry. But what procedure should be followed to discover this element which gives form to the poem? Reduction is undoubtedly the method which will necessarily lead to the *Poe'S* as its end result; the latter appears implicitly or explicitly as a maxim or proverb. (López Sevillano, "Introduction" xvii)

The *Poe'S* as an implicit maxim can be seen in the following poem:

> [He would have wanted to die sobbed child
> for whom, omnipotent, he did it.
> I am utopia that bleeds drop by drop
> in sound that indivisible
>
> is sometimes unpronounceable]

Querría morir niño sollozado
por quien, omnipotente, lo hizo.
Soy utopía que desangra
en sonido que indivisible

es a veces impronunciable.
(Balcón a la bahía 44)

This poem's implicit maxim can be stated in the following terms:

An understanding of All Things as Thought-forms in the mind of God, the infinite spirit. Thus as genetic metaphysics so clearly points out, what is held in the Mind of God or the Absolute *Is*, constitutes all there is outside of God himself.

God is not, however, simply the matter from which the material things and creatures of the world are created. He is a spiritual being of a finer substance, perhaps similar in a certain sense to what we call consciousness or mind but elevated to the realm of the eternal, the ominiscient, the omnipotent. Thus in this short poem the "sound" of God's mind *(utopía)* is indivisible and unspeakable *(impronunciable)* but nevertheless more real than anything man can create. The mystical conception of genetics is that in the infinite mind of God, where man dwells, there is only Life, and there can be no Death.

Thus we see the intimate link between the *Poe'S* and the principle of relation which is central to the genetic conception of metaphysics. As Rielo writes in his unpublished essay *Introduction to My Thought, in relatione omnia revelantu*r": "The appetite for relation responds to a peremptory necessity that, at the same time, is the basis of culture." (n. pag.) Relation, then, is a fundamental and spontaneous fact of our natural experience of the world in which we live. Basing his metaphysics on this fact, Rielo concludes that "this absolute relational principle is the genetic principle" (López Sevillano, *Pure Metaphysics* 205).

This genetic principle keeps man always safe from harm even if he leaves his mortal body behind. What is truly him, his essence, is "relational" with the God the Absolute, and therefore "immortal" in the ultimate sense of the word. Thus the *Poe'S* subjects language to its own dynamic; the language of the *Poe'S* remains constantly in touch with a unitary truth despite the paradoxicial multiplicity of that truth's forms of expression. The following stanza explores this paradox:

[You give me your hand without possible affinity
with the infinite that You are, You alone.
That is why, your happiness does not break this being of mine
that lives in spite of death.]

Tú me das la mano sin afinidad posible
con el infinito que Tú eres, Tú sólo.
Por eso, tu alegría no quiebra este ser mío
que vive a pesar de la muerte.
(*Pasión y muerte* 29)

The constitutive truth of the *Poe'S* is that there can be only one God, only one perfect, infinite, absolute being. Finite man must work through life towards God's perfection. The paradox is of course that man's individual smallness and unimportance do not rob him of his destiny, which is his immortality in spirit and life in God his Father and creator, for the universe in which he lives is held in the mind of God.

As the *Idente* scholars have shown in detailed analyses of individual poems by Rielo, the *Poe'S* operates as a determining force even at the level of style in Rielo's work. One example of its operation appears in Rielo's abundant use of neologisms, which function for Rielo as part of the unitive process in the form and in the content of his poetry. When Rielo compounds two ordinary words into one new word, such as ["sweetsad"] *dulcetriste* or ["bluesoul"] *almazul*, he unites the ordinary words with bonds of communality and achieves a synthesis of their semantic--and often their sonoric--elements. The *Idente* critics call this practice the "nominal noumenic." A second stylistic practice through which the *Poe'S* is manifested in Rielo's poetry is his unconventional use of grammar and punctuation to heighten the poetry's conceptual value. As López Sevillano writes:

He does not, therefore, strictly submit himself to grammatical rules. Let us give an example: "Nació ha... la mañana/que la tarde se llevara." The ha... may be rendered by means of the prepositions por, con, a, desde, hacia ... la mañana: that is, this expression manifests the pluriform content of a state between "life" and "non life" which cannot be reduced to either. This original construction by the author may be understood through analogy to the way in

54

which the transition from late afternoon to nightfall is conceived--that time at which it is neither day nor night and which, we believe, cannot be expressed by any specific noun in the Spanish language. (Introduction xix)

Closely related to the *Poe'S* as well is an aspect of Rielo's technique that I call "densification": the compacting of multiple and expansive meanings into very few words. This technique appears most obviously in Rielo's shorter lyrics, but sometimes may be found as well in his longer, more prosaic poems. In the beautiful poem that concludes *Balcón a la bahía* this technique is evident:

[Why not remain
flesh alone?

Christ:

Your truth, impeccable; your poetry, weightless.
You separated the light from the shadow, life from death.
The poets gather that which you for different fires have separated.
Lashes are their poems for just storm:

History of misfortune,
Embalmed death by ice.
Myth of sand and of caterpillar.

Already none dies, is dying, is dead.
We are dead men on earth of dead men.
Shadows that an inextinguishable wind passes through
On nights fermented by winter.

Men know nothing of your death.
Nor of leaving the cathedral of the moment.
They are only inert dream behind a window glass.
At the end, nothing, nothing...

Dead men wrapping themselves in their ashes.
If perhaps, scuba divers of an occult sex.
Narcissus sucking milk of clay.
Revivalness, and not life, of the abandoned tree
This is all the faith that they comprehended.

And you Christ, for this only have you died?]

¿Por qué no quedar
la carne a solas?

Cristo:

Tu verdad, impecable; tu poesía, ingrávida.
Separaste la luz de la tiniebla, la vida de la muerte.
Los poetas reúnen lo que tú para fuegos diferentes has separado.
Látigos son sus poemas para justo tormento:

Historia de desdicha,
Embalsamada muerte por el hielo.
Mito del polvo y de la oruga.

Ya nadie muere: se muere, es muerto.
Somos muertos en tierra de muertos.
Sombras que un viento inextinguible traslada
en noches fermentadas por el invierno.

Los hombres nada saben de tu muerte.
Ni dejar la catedral del instante.
Sólo son sueño inerte detrás de una vidriera.
Al final, nada, nada...

Muertos enredándose en su ceniza.
Si acaso, buceadores de un sexo oculto.
Narcisos mamando leche de arcilla.
Reviviscencia, que no vida, de árbol abandonado.
Esta es toda la fe que comprendieron.

¿Y tú, Cristo, para esto sólo has muerto?
(67)

Densification occurs in the opening of the poem with the line "why
not remain \ flesh alone?"--which immediately opens the wide range
of implications raised by the possibility of a "life" on a different level
than the level of the body and the five senses. Another example of this
technique appears in the line "Embalmed death by ice"--which refers
to modern man's lack of feelings, his incapacity for positive emotional

experience, and to the multiple and diverse consequences that this "ice" or coldness has had for him and his world. A final example is "Myth of sand and of caterpillar." The sands of the desert that blow and cover all, the sands in which the ostrich hides its head, seem to be opposed within the "myth" elaborated here to the caterpillar, whose extraordinary life is one of total reversal, total metamorphosis: he changes from a crawling, earth-bound creature into a being that flies in the air and drinks the nectar of flowers. The butterfly, we should also note, was the symbol of *psyche* or the soul in ancient Greek myth. This technique of densification provides one of the means by which Rielo resolves the paradox implicit in the multiple expressions language makes available for a single and unitary truth.

Perhaps López Sevillano best sums up the force of the *Poe'S* in Rielo's work in his claim that, "To the mystical poet, God is always the subject of reference" (Introduction xix). Uniting poetry's essence to a divine essence, the *Poe'S* thus makes the poet's aesthetic practice something akin to Christ's miraculous resurrection:

> [The mystical poet's] mission, truly lofty in this world, is to liberate the physical aesthetically from its pathology of ugliness. Whoever laments, protests, curses, or vituperates is not, strictly speaking, a poet, since, by aggravating the ugly, he does not proceed towards its aesthetic cure. Christ, the mystical poet *par excellence*, does not diminish the value of the flesh, but rather, transforms it into a state of aesthetic resurrection which enables it to be known as it is known by God. It is God who inspires poetry; the mystical life is poetry, and the poem is one of its concrete moments. In the measure in which the poet is faithful to it, he will sing the praises of the whole of nature and of the human spirit, which is its summit]. (López-Sevillano, Introduction xix)

Through the *Poe'S*, then, Rielo integrates the mystical notion of union with the divine into the very techniques of his poetry. As Santiago Acosta, Aldo Forés, and *Idente* critics have shown, this notion is also integrated fully into his poetry's thematic content through three key features drawn from the classical tradition of mysticism: the "convivium" or banquet where God and the poet feast; the dialogue state; and a feeling of destiny or fate. The "convivium" has a universal tradition and can be traced back to the *Song of Songs*. We recall the mystical night of grapes; the room with ornamental, elaborate decorations; the bride's excitement just before her husband's arrival;

57

and, finally, the *agape* or banquet of love. In the New Testament, the banquet idea is also found: Christ shares supper with the Apostles before his death, and once arisen, he dines with them. A passage from the *Song of Songs* may thus serve to introduce the convivium as it appears in Rielo's poetry, especially in *Llanto azul:* "... eat, O friends; drink, yea, drink abundantly, O beloved" (5:1). The soul's state of mind while expectantly participating in the meeting is expressed in strikingly original imagery in the poem by Rielo titled "*Ciudad hallada*" ["A City Found"]:

[Here I am.
A city dreamed, blue trees that never fall.
Pushed.
As by the wind or by the stomping sea.
And nude and pure the mountain attacks; it then falls
defeated in the shaded valley.
        Hush, foliage, be quiet!
        It's time for Him to pass just like He always does.
        Dressed in green leaves
        that cover Him.]

Aquí estoy.
Ciudad soñada en árboles azules que no caen.
Empujado.
Como hace el viento como el mar que pisa.
Y a la montaña ataca, desnudo y puro, para caer vencido
en el valle umbrío.
        ¡Callad, oh frondas, callad!
        es hora que El pase como lo hace siempre.
        Vestido de verdes hojas
        que lo cubren.
                (*Llanto azul* 20)

    Kisses are the symbol of the mystical food at this banquet which Father and son, God and poet, arrange for each other, a banquet consummated in ecstasy. Sometimes, in Rielo's early poetry with its strong element of Mariolatry, the kiss is offered to or solicited from a beloved woman reminiscent of those who appear in the *Song of Songs*:

[Blow me a kiss
into the water,
Beloved lady,
And you will see me
dive deep down,
like a port urchin.]

Echame un beso
al agua,
Amada mía,
Verás cómo buceo
hasta el fondo,
como un golfo de puerto.

(Dios y árbol 67)

In later poetry, however, the kiss always comes from the Father. It is charged with ecstatic values, among them the painful struggle of ridding the self of "self"--an experience which is a necessary step in contemplation. In "Mi mar" ["My Sea"], Sea is a metaphor of ecstasy, while salt symbolizes the afflicted state that accompanies the sweetness of the kiss, the contact with the beloved being:

Give me your salt, O sea. Anoint my lips
so that they will kiss bittersweet,
lost among the blue, ascending in your water
like rising wings that pass,
now anxious, now serene,
above your waves, O sea, among daydreams
of other kisses my celestial
beloved navigates at me, sea wolf
salt-toughened, sealed in blue, and wrapped in breezes.
They're living all our loving hours.
Like you O sea you who subsist in sky.

Dame oh mar tu sal. Unge mis labios
para que besen dulcemente amargos,
perdidos entre azules, ascendentes en tus aguas,
como alas que suben,
que transcurren,
ya agitadas, ya serenas,

59

por tus ondas oh mar entre sueños despiertos
a otros besos que me navega
mi celestial amado, lobo de mar
en sales curtido, sellado su azul, de brisas cubierto.
Ellos viven nuestras horas amantes.
Como tú oh mar que en el cielo subsistes.

(*Llanto azul* 28)

Keeping this kiss pure will consume all the poet's attention. Purity demands sweetness and bitterness, as the poem reveals. The preservative properties of salt make it the most appropriate image for keeping all the virtualities of the love-banquet intact. One notes that there is nothing sexual about this intimate relationship between the lovers, and the poet rejects any carnal interpretation of the kiss--not because he considers it degrading, but because it de-virtualizes the heavenly nature of the kiss:

[Oh kiss, please, do not dress yourself in flesh.
          Flesh annoys me.
Be breeze for me instead... She walks
          just everywhere.
And though she savorless, she does have
          exactly what you're lacking.
She crosses the destiny...
          that you can not.

Beso, por favor, no te vistas de carne.
          La carne me fastidia.
Séme de brisa... Ella camina
          a todas partes.
Y, aunque a nada sabe, tiene
          de lo que tú careces.
Cruza el destino...
          que tú no puedes

("Beso, por favor" ["A Kiss, please"], *Dios y árbol* 81)

The kiss is a mystical touch that turns into rapt caresses of love, a state of being in which the poet becomes so sensitive to divine affect that he feels he is dying. Death herein is a figure expressing the moments of an emotional inflammation that fragile human nature can barely endure:

[When you touch me, o my God,
you're always wearing gloves,
and yet I still complain
Because I feel a pain
of suede
I'm anguished and I want to die...]

Cuando me tocas, Dios mío,
siempre lo haces con guante,
y sin embargo yo me lamento.
Es que siento un dolor
de ante
que me acongoja y muero...
("Cuando me tocas, Dios mío" 73)

And again we see:

[Ecstasy, do not rip
my poor eyelid open
just because it can't
stand up to you.
Don't leave, either.
Your presence is all
that I live...
Beyond even air.]

Extasis, no rompas
mi pobre párpado,
sólo porque no puede
resistirte.
Tampoco te marches.
Tu estancia es todo
lo que vivo...
más allá del aire.
("... no rompas", *Noche clara* 99)

This feasting with divine love, sharing a table with the Father himself, does not make the poet a creature displaced or withdrawn into his own little world of eminence. This is a moment when solidarity with human beings crystallizes into poems of lamentation, when the poet meditates on the low esteem in which people hold the exquisite treasures of mystical love and the "kisses of the breeze":

[Just how much love piles up like trash
each night in front of every doorway.
Yes. How many kisses weeping throwaway,
torn from their lips, which say goodbye
to life from rubber cubes.
Yet none of them will ever return.
And knowing that it shall repeat with you,
morning kiss, because that's a tradition
that dates to yesterdays before the centuries.]

Cuánto amor como basura se amontona
en portal de cada casa y cada noche.
Sí. Cuántos besos como restos lloran
de sus labios desgajados, que dicen adiós
a la vida desde sus cubos de goma.
Ninguno vuelve, ninguno.
Y saber que se repetirá contigo, beso
del mañana, porque ésta es la costumbre
que nació tan ayer... que no tiene siglo.
                    ("Amor como basura" ["Love piles up like trash"],
                    Pasión y muerte 79)

The second classically mystical thematic element that the *Idente* scholars have identified in Rielo's poetry is the dialogue between the participants in the love-exchange. Santiago Acosta explains that this "dialogue factor" starts with a type of courtly-love phrase: "thou hast deceived me" (Jr. 20:7). One precedent is found in the *Song of Songs*: "Set me as a seal upon thine heart, as a seal upon thine arm" (8:6). Another appears in the New Testament account of the prodigal son returning from his wanderings and being embraced by his father, who issues the following order: "Bring forth the best robe, and put it on him; and put a ring on his hand, and shoes on his feet: And bring hither the fatted calf, and kill it; and let us eat, and be merry" (Luke 15: 22-23). The poems of San Juan de la Cruz also engage in dialogue with the Husband, and the Husband with his soul: "And you were married to me there, / There I gave you my hand" (23). In Rielo's work, this dialogue element is found in abundance:

62

[As yesterday...
as today...
as always. Even if there's a lot of dying
under heaven.
You, Son, will remain
with your wings alive and open.
Revolving. Around me. As always
it has been
and always will be.
I promise you.]

Como ayer...
como hoy...
como siempre. Aunque haya mucho morir
debajo del cielo.
Tú, hijo, permanecerás
con tus alas vivas y abiertas.
En giro. En torno mío. Como siempre
ha sido
y será siempre.
Yo te lo prometo.
(Llanto azul 32)

The third classically mystical thematic element defined by the
Idente scholars is the presence of destiny or fate. Together with the
images of house, temple, mountain, and the Promised Land, this
presence determines the internal dynamics of the Old Testament: "I
held him, and would not let him go, until I had brought him into my
mother's house" (Song of Solomon, 3:4). Indeed, the temple, the
house, the mountain, and the Promised Land are all images of destiny
or fate, which is also internalized in the New Testament as follows: "...
true worshippers shall worship the Father in spirit and in truth" (John
4:23). In classic Spanish mysticism, the presence of fate or destiny is
manifested as a vehement desire to achieve the contemplative state of
seeing God: "Soul, what do you want from me? / Just to see you, O my
God," "See how I pine to see you, / And my pain is so complete / That
I am dying because I cannot die" exclaims Santa Teresa (Obras... 499).
Rielo, however, adds something new to classic mysticism. His anxiety
concerning fate or destiny is not directed at merely seeing God, but at
total oneness, total possession:

[My fate is, oh, to blend within your bowels
becoming re-created being beyond all loneliness
oblivion steps upon while climbing zenith-paths.
No. What I anguish for is not just seeing you,
my prize for the lashes I have suffered....
Don't olive-trees feel that way about olives,
and isn't that what love is like when born?
My God: oh may my ohs awaken me this way!]

Mi destino es, ay, viscerarme contigo,
recrearme, ser más allá de toda soledad
que el olvido atropelle en su cenital camino.
No. No es sólo verte, como premio del látigo
que he sufrido, lo que yo ansío...
¿No es así acaso la aceituna para el olivo
y no es así el amor cuando ha nacido...?
Dios mío: ¡que mi aye así me despierte!
                ("Más que verte" ["Not Just Seeing You"]
                Paisaje desnudo 129)

The seal in the *Song of Songs* has, in Fernando Rielo's poetics, become "blending within bowels." Such blending is a total oneness, a vital unit, just as the human and divine natures are blended within the person of Christ. This concept of mystical enclosure appears again in "Día Claro" ["Clear Day"] where God says: "My breast is thine!" (*Llanto azul* 77).

In both classical mystical poetry and Rielo's work, the idea of destiny is closely linked to certain concepts of time and space. One notes that the Old Testament introduces the concept of space with images such as houses, mountains, and temples; it also adds the dimension of time, which means that the sequence of destiny implies displacement in space and a subsequent inversion of time. In the New Testament, the categories of time and space disappear as soon as Christ defines man and his destiny or fate as a function of ecstasy, in other words, "in spirit and in truth." The mystics of Spain's classic period, however, still retain a certain tendency to define relation between the contemplating mystic and the object of his contemplation in spatial terms. Rielo, by contrast, as the *Idente* scholars point out, consciously places himself outside the categories of space and time by making possession the fundamental condition of his poetry.

Possession excludes states such as searching and anxiety; no climbing up mountains and shores a la San Juan de la Cruz (although both mountains and shores have a heavily symbolic meaning in Rielo), but rather ownership and blending. This makes the poet say, "I do not pursue my destiny. / For I already have it" ("Irnos" ["Going"] *Pasión y muerte* 68). This ownership of destiny has of course not yet been consummated; only the "Father-son" model can furnish it with its full meaning. Such a model is removed from a static or quietistic interpretation of the mystical experience. Love achieves its resolution in successive augmentations of the mystic's state of being, within which the mystic appropriates within himself both God and God's creation as an intimate and private landscape.

In tracing Rielo's relation to the traditions of mysticism, one cannot ignore either Rielo's philosophical comments on mysticism or his theoretical comments on poetry. In Rielo's philosophy, man is defined as a function of God. In other words, God defines man by uniting with him from the first moment of his existence by means of an absolute act; thus man is infused with filial essence. Rielo's view, then, is that man is born into a mystical condition of union with God that can be augmented or decreased during the course of his lifetime in accordance with his moral behavior and the development of his essence and consciousness. Far from being accidental, man's filial character is in fact his essential definition (Rielo, "Definición" n. pag.).

Rielo's view that man is born into a mystical condition is reflected in his corresponding view that poetry is fundamentally "mystical consciousness":

Poetry is the mystical consciousness of humanity, but much more than just a critical consciousness: rather than a treatise denouncing errors, it is in fact an evocation of sobs. Yes, a poet's vocation is weeping, not engaging in discussions with mankind." (Rielo, "Concepción genética..." n. pag.)

In a speech read during the Fourth European Poetry Festival, Rielo reaffirms the essentially mystical nature of poetry when he states: "... so-called 'mystic poetry' is nothing more than an eminent re-creation within poetry of a poet's state of moved tenderness when the strings of his lyre trap their creator or the Absolute between them..." ("Poesía y mística" 32). This quotation confirms the thesis that a mystic poet mounts his words within the setting of his certainty that he is within

God. Rielo clarified this point in responding to a question at the same gathering about the difference between his poetry and that of Juan Ramón Jiménez:

[The difference is probably that in Juan Ramón Jiménez, God is a function of desire and is characterized by a search for a God whom he desires because he does not possess. I am not searching for this God, as I already have Him; rather, He is a Father, and I need consummation with Him.] ("Comentario..." n. pag.)

This poetics of possession marks a crucial difference between Rielo's work and other modern poetry that bears mystical qualities, such as that of Gabriel Celaya and Blas de Otero, in which transcendental anxiety is often combined with a commitment to man's social problematic. Rielo, whose speeches and writings have repeatedly demonstrated his basic preoccupation with the profound crisis modern societies are undergoing, nevertheless surprises the reader with the "purity" of his verse, with its unswerving dedication to the lyric re-creation of his filial bond with God and other transcendental themes. In the "Note to Readers" in *Dios y árbol*, he writes:

[My poetry has one theme, whose magnitude makes it single and permanent. The theme: destiny or fate, which we insist on relegating to the back burner, preferring to invoke many others which, by nature, cannot define us, although it is true that they are capable of harassing us. Someone is subject to our loving fate which not even death can close off.] (5)

These ideas endow Rielo's poetry with a sense of solidity that stands in sharp contrast with the ambiguous and unstable expressions often found in modern poetic texts exposed to the aesthetic influences of other arts, such as painting. The latter have often fragmented artistic issues and inculcated a sharp skepticism regarding the substance of poetry, which makes it easy to view a poem as mere artifact. The idea that a poetic work of art is a viable instrument for achieving union with the Creator or God, and that it is a true receptacle wherein the light of the absolute Act reverberates, doubtlessly contains a heavy dose of romanticism. However, it seems not to have suffered all the tumult which is presently shaking theoretical concepts about literature and even language itself. Though not monolithically established in critical consciousness, the notion that poetry is fictitious territory and imaginary discourse is nevertheless very prevalant. It brings to mind Plato's distrust of art as being twice removed from reality. George Steiner argues in *Language and Silence* that the cruel manipulation to which words have been subjected in modern totalitarian regimes, as well as the inability to use them to express the magnitude of World War II horrors, have made language a minefield of insecurity (150).

Rielo's poetry, in opposition to the modern skepticism about language, places full trust in words and the scope of their comprehensive power:

> [You, poetry, are my true feeling.
> You are like some profound evening philosophy
> that sweetens rustic tones in all that shouts.
>
> Tú eres, poesía, mi sentimiento verdadero.
> Eres como la honda filosofía de la tarde
> que dulcifica el tono agreste de todo lo que grita.]
> ("Inocencia amante" ["Loving Innocence"],
> *Noche clara* 63)

Rielo has profound respect for the word. He has introduced his poetry with the verse from the Gospel of John that says: "In the beginning was the word and the word was with God and the word was God" (John 1:1). In one of the *Ateneos* he holds on Sundays at the idente school in Tenerife, he quoted the poet Dag Hammarskjold:

> "Respect for the word" is the first commandment in the discipline which a man can be educated to maturity, intellectual, emotional, and moral.
> Respect for the word--to employ it with scrupulous care and an incorruptible heartfelt love of truth --is essential if there is to be any growth in a society or in the human race.
> To misuse the word is to show contempt for man. It undermines the bridges and poisons the wells. It causes man to regress down the long path of his evolution.
> "But I say unto you, that every idle word that men speak..."
> (Hammarskjold 112)

In Rielo's poems words are given in perfect consummation of the message to a waiting world. The poet has admitted the deep-seated romanticism of his work, recognizing the authority therein to be none other than that of intense emotional feeling. The mark of his romanticism is total freedom. Such romanticism becomes the means by which his poetry gains the freedom to ascend from the outward material world to the higher world, which is also the inner, invisible mystic world where man becomes one with God and one with the world.

If Rielo's work challenges the skepticism of much modern poetry, however, it does not pose its challenge by simply returning to the paradigms of classical Spanish mystical poetry, such as that of San Juan de la Cruz and Santa Teresa de Jesús. Dámaso Alonso sees in the works of both saints a process of divinization of traditional and courtly lyrics, unless of course he alludes to a more ancient and universal source, the *Song of Songs* (Alonso, *Poetas*... 219). In Rielo however, the poetic word is not derived primarily from transforming classic models. His poems are profoundly modern, as can be confirmed by noting that the aesthetic blueprint used is a novel one which makes a decisive turn from the metaphorical direction inherited from St. Teresa and St. John. The latter generally make use of sexual and matrimonial images in order to indicate the exquisite quality and intimacy of a love-relationship between man and God. The axis of Rielo's poetic vision, on the other hand, is the filial relationship between Father and Child, which forms the fundamental basis of his genetic concept of the nature of mankind. For Rielo, man is essentially a "child of God." Rielo's work is thus bereft of sexual connotations, revealing instead the vast expressive possibilities derived from the poet's filial certainty.

Rielo's work also shuns the didacticism evident in the long poems of San Juan de la Cruz. One result of San Juan's pedagogical intent--his wish to describe the operations performed by the godhead within an ascetic soul walking the path of perfection--is a depersonalization which sometimes burdens his poetry. San Juan was no doubt conditioned by the principles of scholasticism, and even by fear of censure from the Holy See, which often functioned as a damper on the free expression of mystical feeling. Consistent with his romantic sensibilities, Rielo makes no attempt at self-effacement; rather, he resolutely positions himself within his verse, unafraid of provoking critical voices which might decry the presence of a creative personality within a work as "aggressive." Rielo nourishes such personal expression by means of the entire gamut of states constituting the makeup of his filial spirit.

Rather than the classical Spanish mystical poets, it is such romantic and modern poets as Gustavo Adolfo Bécquer, Juan Ramón Jiménez, and Vicente Aleixandre that constitute the major literary influences completely assimilated within Rielo's artistic language. From such poets Rielo has gained certain convictions about the importance of both inclusiveness and inward self-exploration in poetry:

> [Mystical poetry excludes nothing. Like love, it includes everything from an incipient sex to a dying wheat-field. Drawing its map requires the geography of an entire soul.]
> ("Poesía y mística" 32)

Another decisively modern aspect of Rielo's poetry is its deployment of a literary language that restores mystical feelings to poetry from decidedly modern sources.[1] He has produced his poems within the currents of present-day poetry, whose vocabulary incorporates words and experiences which other eras rejected as "non-poetic." Fixing one's focus primarily upon the mystical relationship between Creator and created might seem to imply an *a priori* limitation of lexical and imagistic possibilities, a limitation polarized in the direction of the subtle area of spiritual realities. Quite the contrary, Rielo's verse derives nourishment from every kind of life-link, finding in virtually any vocuabulary or range of images a means of invoking his own powerful penetration by divine love. In the following fragment of "Dios mío" ["My God"], one observes the poet as he traces the parameters of divine reality by means of the language of psychiatry as a suggestive contrast to lyrical, religious background voices:

> [My God:
> You are not an idea within my thirsty mind,
> nor some syndrome of my nervous system.
> No, beloved nightingale, you are an ecstasy
> that you whistle while you follow me...
> and I have no more foliage to hide myself.]

---

1. Consider, for example these words spoken by the French poet Alain Bosquet at the presentation of Fernando Rielo's literary work in Paris, on November 2, 1984: ["One could achieve transcendence dressing in a perfectly knotted tie. In this sense, it could be that redemption is the most vital and necessary road: a Christianity not built up out of strict dogmas but rather of mysticism, so that the latter might not be considered as a disassociation from the contemporary world..."]

> Dios mío:
> Tú no eres idea en mi mente sedienta
> ni un síndrome de mi sistema nervioso.
> Tú eres, mi ruiseñor amado, éxtasis que me silbas
> persiguiéndome...
> y ya no tengo fronda donde ocultarme.
>
> *(Paisaje desnudo* 62)

In addition to the diversity of its language and images, Rielo's work also displays a wide range of emotional tonalities. It resolutely acknowledges the pain and anarchy of human life, even while taking as its fundamental principle a thirst for consummation with the Absolute. The consciousness involved here is thus both joyful and afflictive, but never hopeless:

> [It suffices to look at ourselves
> in order to laugh a little.
> At least I laugh
> but wind up crying.
> And when you leave?
> Oh God, then I shall exist alone.]

> Basta contemplarnos
> para reír un poco.
> Yo al menos río
> para acabar llorando.
> ¿Y cuando te alejas...?
> Entonces, oh Dios, sólo existo.

> ("Si te alejas" ["If you leave"] 107)

In spite of a trace of levity in Fernando Rielo's short poems, they nevertheless entail an expressive gravity which lends tension to the poetry's tissue of words. The tight dialectics of laughter and weeping are by no means paradoxical, since laughter and weeping reflect the chromaticism of the filial relationship and its confrontation with existence. Through God's mediation, indeed, laughter and weeping become the quintessence of being in the world. It is through filial consciousness, the consciousness of one's origin and destiny, as Rielo argues, that the pain and sense of failure of earthly existence may be transformed into a higher, more joyful state of being:

[I am sure I am fairly correct when I define the human person as being someone-with-a-consciousness-of-someone.]
("Poesía y Mística" 28)

[... Poetry is this objective consciousness of someone absolute who has stewardship of the ideal form of our existence in such a manner that our real, living self walks and becomes transported in the direction of its final consummation in conformity with this other module of our existence-within-the-world; until such time, however, we live in perplexity and pain.] (30-1)

Mystical poetry carries a bliss beyond religion, namely the possession of God, which produces an elevation in one's level of being and consciousness. Such possession is of course relative within this phenomenological world, and only those who come in contact with esoteric teaching, and then put that teaching into practice, can transform themselves and fulfill their potential in God's experiment. Thus a certain sorrow attends the state of possession fundamental to the existence of the lyric subject of Rielo's poems. For the love of God alone cannot achieve the complete satisfaction desired; not even divine contemplation can quench the thirst for a "consummated union" or change of Being:

[I cannot settle for merely gazing at you
when I become exempt from death.
However beautiful that gaze may be,
my soul would still be sad, O God.]

No me conformo con sólo verte
cuando exento de la muerte quede.
Si bella sería la mirada,
mi alma, ay, quedaría triste.
("Más que verte," *Paisaje desnudo* 129)

It is that the poetry of religious doubt and challenge is aesthetically more profitable than the poetry of faith. Rielo's work, however, evidences that using union with God as a poetic springboard need not result in a sentimental lyricism in which dramatic human feeling becomes tame. Mystical poetry should not be confused with pietism. Mystical feeling moves man's entire being, from his existential fragility to his most illustrious eternal destiny or fate. One need not exclude

71

from it any thematic or formal element. A poem such as "Vírgenes mundos" ["Virgin Worlds"] is simultaneously a mystical testimony of a heavenly city and a portrait of a worldly city, complete with time-bound social changes:

[Year 40 died or passed. Nothing's changed.
The pulpit's quiet... just in case. Successful council.
More priestly garb now hangs than underwear on terraces.
Boys and girls in multitudes wearing tight rags.
And everything seems small and abstract. Science, art.
A sandwich, even sex.
The poet Breeze has found a job: she cleans
the safety-valves of heaven with her foam detergent.
Yes. The Breeze no longer whispers heaven's kisses;
the Breeze's trademark was reduced in price
she earns her keep by working weekdays now.
The sun is just another neighbor, even though the most
distinguished.
That's what the neighbors say when constantly reminding him
about the day he wasn't there.
The poet used to call the moon Dear Moon. Today she's just a
bloodhound 'mong the dirty rags
which night conceals and tells no one about.
Stars look like cats that hunt on roofs and balconies.
The town demands a poem of expenses
if you've been walking 'round it for a while.]

Año 40 ha muerto o ha pasado. Es lo mismo.
El púlpito ha callado... por si acaso. Un concilio cumplido.
Hay ya más sotanas colgadas que bragas en las terrazas.
Chicos y chicas con trapos ceñidos en multitud hermosa.
Todo parece muy pequeño. Todo abstracto, la ciencia, el arte,
el sandwich y hasta el sexo.
La poetisa brisa ya tiene empleo. Su tarea, limpiar el cielo
de tubos de escape con su jabón de espuma.
Sí. La brisa ya no susurra ósculos celestes;
la brisa es marca barata
que en horas laborables trabaja.
El sol es un vecino más. El más distinguido, sin duda.
Lo dicen los vecinos cuando tanto le citan el día que falta.
Luna lunita la llamó el poeta. Hoy es la sabuesa de los trapos sucios

72

que la noche oculta y a nadie cuenta.
Las estrellas parecen gatos a la caza de terrazas o tejados.
Hay un poema de gastos que la ciudad exige
al cabo del rato de caminar por ella.

> (*Llanto azul* 44)

The town in question is a crowded twentieth-century city--hard to live in, polluted, anti-bucolic, the last place anyone would expect to make contact with transcendence. God Himself, however, has invited the poet for a walk:

[Evening. The light diminishes. Things turn lackluster. Flies don't
>> buzz.
My Father lives eternal in the heavens, and now
Invites me to go out into the street.
>> I fling
>> Me out.]

Tarde. La luz declina. Las cosas se opacan. Las moscas, taciturnas.
Mi Padre que eterno en el cielo vive
me anima a salir a la calle.
>> A ella
>> me tiro.   (45)

This impersonal city-space lends itself to contemplation, contemplation resulting in a city transfigured--streets, residents, and all--into an eternal town wherein the poet sees his own home:

[Within such moments of waking dreams, how much
I loved the life you placed into my life: a life of a thousand
>> universes,
with brand-new streets and squares, and with new heavens
I promptly flew through using all my wings!
Enormous worlds, enormous, with enormous waters
within enormous skies, where delicate immortal forms would
>> greet me
and not leave me. Skies full of dogs immortal and immortal fishes,
birds immortal, and fleshless zenith breeze so pure, so lovely,
so shining that I cannot speak or act...
...
I reached the homes, I saw the homes as well...
I saw my own, composed of brilliances. I didn't lookinside.

But I did see the doors... Bright stars in mid-air halt, perpetual
ecstasy.
I kissed it, feeling so beside myself I couldn't even weep.
O Father, I could not, among those many loving beings.]

¡Cuánto quise en esos instantes de mi sueño despierto
la vida que en mi vida pusiste: una vida de mil universos
con nuevas calles, con nuevas plazas, con nuevos cielos
que yo recorrí con todas mis alas!
Oh mundos, mundos inmensos de inmensas aguas
en inmensos cielos que inmortales formas, ingrávidas, me
acogieron
sin dejarme. Cielos con inmortales perros, inmortales peces,
inmortales aves, cenitales aires sin carne, tan puros, tan bellos,
tan brillantes que ni decir ni hacer yo puedo.
(...)
A las moradas llegué, las moradas vi...
También la mía, de brillos hecha. No la vi por dentro.
Sí sus puertas... de luceros detenidos éxtasis perpetuos.
La besé tan fuera de mí que ni llorarme pude.
Oh Padre, no pude entre tantos seres amantes.   (45)

The poet creates an immense space of contemplation, of
meditation, in this poem: "enormous worlds, enormous, with enormous
waters / within enormous skies." In order for the transformation of
being in the mystic experience to occur, the center in man, which
normally operates by focussing on the senses and the material world,
must lie very quiet. When this center in man is absorbed and
disssolved, a space is created where something else can operate,
something sacred that originates beyond the images built by thought.
This immense space is produced meditatively, contemplatively, by
mind emptying itself of mind. It is a movement between the known and
the unknown, which mysteriously connects with love: not
pleasure-seeking or sexual love, but deep, purified, imageless love, the
love that in this poem is called "perpetual ecstasy."

The weeping and pain that express Rielo's sense of relative
possession deserve further exploration. Rielo himself defines this pain
as originating in one's consciousness of the contradiction between
love's unity and the heterogeneity of mundane life--"While we pass

through this world, the oneness of love accentuates the faraway" or in one's consciousness of one's fallen state:

[From Thee, Father, yes, from Thee did I descend
Just like a bolt that cracks the ground....]

De Ti, Padre; sí, de Ti he descendido como caído rayo
que el suelo rompe....
("Mi creación amada" ["My Beloved Creation"] 48)

As a "deep-rooted" poet, Rielo does not imply through his images of weeping and pain that he considers himself mistreated, as though someone were raining blows on him from above. The introduction to *Llanto azul* underscores that the poet's sobs are not an insoluble problem, but just another value of the unitive state: sob and smile marry, and this marriage constitutes the essence of being. Neither sob nor smile could exist without the other (López Sevillano, Introduction vii).

The necessity of suffering and its relationship to the development of higher states of consciousness is a constant theme in both Rielo and the classic mystics. Like the classic mystics, Rielo's lyric subject feels "wounded" by God--that is, "wounded" by Love--which makes his sadness pleasant:

[Brightness never comes all by herself.
Sadness keeps her company, no doubt.
Insistent sadness doesn't try to flee,
but sweetly knocks, and just as sweetly hurts.
However, Sadness isn't sad to excess.
Some days she laughs....]

La claridad nunca viene solitaria.
Le acompaña sin duda la tristeza.
Una tristeza que insiste, que no huye,
que, dulce, golpea; que, dulce, duele.
No es, sin embargo, demasiado triste.

75

Hay días que ríe....
>("La claridad no es solitaria" ["Brightness is not
>Lonely"], *Pasión y muerte* 35)

Deeper than either sob or smile in Rielo's poetry, however, lies the impulse of ecstasy, the center which imparts unity to his poetics. From this configurating center, as I have already argued in examining the theory of the *Poe'S*, Rielo's poetic expression develops like a branching tree. Ecstasy, which Rielo himself characterizes as the "dynamics of our existence" ("Poesía y Mística" 27), is the filter through which all the expressive material poured into a poem must pass; therefore, there are no strategies, no artifice. This explains the highly stylized effect imparted to the forms which constitute Rielo's aesthetic universe. All his poems appear enveloped in an atmosphere of high-temperature lyricism, distilled to their own essence. They transcend their own blunt everyday profiles. The epigones of projective poetry consider a poem a "high-energy construct"; if they are correct, this image is applicable to Rielo's poems. His poetry seems to liberate an energy which envelops his figurative world with a misty veil of purity and timelessness. The impulse of ecstasy raises his poetic forms to a higher level of reality.

Rielo's poems involve a never-ending organic process of decanting and connecting which rejects or transmutes anything incoherent, disintegrated, or irrational. His poetry speaks to us of a comprehensive feeling of the whole of the universe and its faults. One is inclined to picture his poetry as a heavenly eye scanning the hidden faces of human tragedy and joy as God might see them. The elements of his cosmic configuration are transformed into a separate poetic landscape where they are simultaneously evaluated and purified of the dross of gloom, necrophilia, and organic decomposition through which many modern poetic works of the existential variety, such as García Lorca's *Poeta en Nueva York* [A Poet in New York], figure deeply-felt anxieties about personal and social crises. Rielo's poems appropriate the anguish of the universe, but yet keep it quiet; instead of converting his discourse into missiles hurled at God, he turns it into a hymn sequence, as in the following passages:

>[And I wait. For everything that's silent
>Among the true internal lights:

the ohs of every cry I know.
The cradle desolate, abandoned.
The lonely whining foliage.
The wind when it decides to blow.
The wounded or mis-opened door.]

Y espero. Espero todo aquello que calla
entre lumbres verdaderas, interiores:

el aye de todos los gritos que conozco.
La cuna abandonada y triste.
La fronda solitaria, quejumbrosa.
La puesta en marcha del viento.
La puerta herida o mal abierta.
                    ("Otra Vez" ["Once More"], *Paisaje desnudo* 101)

[Come ye poor fragile, brittle creatures,
I can console you with my own distress.
Come unto that eternal break of day,
my dawn which never shall be cold.]

Venid pobres criaturas quebradizas
que consolaros puedo con la tristeza mía.
Venid al eterno amaneciendo
de mi alba nunca fría.
                    ("Venid a mí" ["Come to Me"] *75)*

Also of importance are the omissions and silences whose
contemplative projection is meant to pour into the poem hope instead
of defeatism, revelation instead of accusation, prayers rather than
rebukes. Ecstasy is the loom upon which each poem is woven, and the
entire elaboration of Rielo's mystical poetry is derived from ecstatic
links. As a result, what is written is the poet's truth. The poem *"Extasis"*
["Ecstasy"] illustrates this premise clearly:

[Oh
     Ecstasy
supremely fresh within my soul so bright,
I cannot even cry... it is all mine.
This sob is language, it is my best friend,
it wants to walk with me in silence now.
     Tell me:
Just how and when did you get in?
I never know. Just that you came from far away.
     Oh.
I cannot hear your steps unless my pulse
collapses and I try to catch it for a moment
with the livid spit of my unfinished shout.
Then I feel lost and simultaneously found
for landscapes new which I cannot describe.
     And
     You.
You with your Infinity open so that I can penetrate,
with wounded love my only impetus of wings.
And that same word as always. Son, you say.
What's son? Something that dreams much more than it demands?
Maybe that name is what the Dawn's been trying
to tell us all these centuries...
and what the wind erases so we yell it out again?
     Oh,
     Ecstasy,
     My only one...
You are the bread of poor men when their soul
and their ambition seek to do with you
what things do with the summer: Live it!]

     Oh
     éxtasis
fresquísimo en alma clarísima,
ya ni puedo llorar... que es lo mío.
Llanto que es lenguaje, el mejor amigo
que pasear conmigo quiere en silencio.
     Dime:
¿Cómo entras que no sé cuándo,
que no sé nunca... sólo que vienes de lejos?

                    Ay.
No siento tus pasos si no es cuando mi pulso
se me derrumba y trato de atraparlo por un instante
con la saliva lívida de mi grito inacabado.
Entonces me siento perdido y a la vez hallado
para nuevas campiñas que describir no puedo.
                    Y
                    Tú,
Tú con tu infinito abierto donde yo pueda penetrarlo
sin más alas que el ímpetu de mi amor herido.
Y como siempre... tu palabra, hijo.
¿Qué es hijo? ¿Algo que sueña más que pide...?
¿Será acaso este nombre lo que nos quiere decir la aurora
desde hace muchos siglos...
y que el viento borra para que lo gritemos de nuevo?
                    Oh
                    éxtasis
                    único...
Tú eres el pan de los pobres cuando su espíritu
su ambición asoma de hacer contigo
lo que las cosas con el verano: ¡vivirlo!   (93)

The cry "Live it!" closing the poem reveals the essence of Rielo's lyricism, which is nourished by deeply personal experience and is thus incapable of being academic in the worst sense of the word. This poem illustrates the basic features of ecstasy: the spirit's extremely pure and virginal condition ("supremely fresh... so bright"); passivity ("my pulse collapses," "I feel lost and simultaneously found"); surprise ("just how and when...?); the movement of complete love ("with wounded love my only impetus of wings"); and a dialogue-situation distanced from the frame of mind of the pure ego ("And that same word as always. Son, you say"). The poem thus evokes a state of mind in which the small "self" as we know it, no longer exists; the thoughts stop. The self is no longer constituted by its memory or experiences, since those are elements of thought. Rather, an awakening of the soul transforms being into something new, something that is part of everything, something that perceives and becomes what is. There is no observer; the observer becomes the observed. This state cannot really be described because words cannot grasp it. The word "God" is not God the Word.

This mystic state can, however, be partially defined by contrasting it with its opposite: "becoming." In "becoming" there is time, the condition of conflict, ambition and desire which keep one imprisoned in the world of thought. The mystic state is not thought, it is not "becoming." One cannot strive for it or go after it or prepare for it according to Rielo. It emerges in the stillness of the inner self when one lets go of thought, lets go of "self," and sees what is. The divine union occurs; a new state of being is achieved; one is part of the whole and the whole is part of the self. It is this "being part of the whole" in its infinite complexity that is the mystic state. All fragmentation ceases and what *is* appears. The essence of this experience is love.

Rielo's poetry reflects this state of oneness of the observer with the observed. We see in his imagery a unitive blending. He is a leaf of the tree that is man; the world around him *is* him; he is part of the universe. Roots descend into the ground; branches ascend into the heavens. Nourishing food--divine love--comes from all sources above and below. The essence of the mystic state is love. These are ancient ideas and can be seen clearly stated in such texts as Plotinus' account of the "dual nature of illumination":

The eye is not wholly dependent upon an outside and alien light; there is an earlier light within itself, a more brilliant light, which it sees sometimes in an momentary flash. At night in the darkness, a gleam leaps from within the eye: or again he makes no effort to see anything; the eyelids close yet a light flashes before us; or we see the eye and it sees the light it contains. This is sight without the act, but it is the real seeing, for it sees light, whereas its other objects were the lit, not the light. It is certainly thus that the spiritual sense ... must have its vision ... not of some other light in some other thing, but of the light within itself, unmingled pure, suddenly gleaming before it, so that we are left wondering whence it came, from within or without; and when it has gone, we say, "It was here. Yet no! it was beyond." But we ought not to question whence; there is no whence, no coming or going in place; now it is seen and now not seen. We must not run after it, but fit ourselves for the vision and then wait tranquilly for its appearance as the eye waits for the rising of the sun, which in its own time appears above the horizon... and gives itself to our sight. (V.I. 586-587)

To Plotinus as to Rielo the beholder is one with the beheld: not a vision encompassed, but a unity comprehended. One understands oneself as part of the unity filled with God.

To know the Divine mind we must study our own soul when it is most God-like; we must put aside the body and the part of the soul that molded the body and the senses with desires and impulses and with every such futility; what is then left is an image of the Divine intellect. Those who are divinely possessed and inspired have at least the knowledge that they hold some great thing within them, though they cannot tell what it is. From the movements that stir them and the utterances that come from them they perceive the power, not themselves, that moves them. (V.II 174-175)

Like Plotinus and like San Juan de la Cruz and the *Upanishads*, Rielo speaks of a state in which one escapes one's finite "self" and in which the Divine Essence is communicated directly from within. This state liberates the mind from its finite anxieties. Like can only apprehend like: when one ceases to be finite, one becomes united with the infinite. In the reduction of the soul to its simplest self, its Divine essence or the "llama de amor viva" ["living flame of love"], one realizes this union, this identity. A change in the level of being occurs. Thus Rielo can only speak of his emotion in terms of God. The discursive mind is incapable of revealing spiritual knowledge, for knowledge depends on being. To know more one must *be* more, one must undergo a transformation which thought alone cannot induce. Being does not change by thought alone, although change may begin with thinking in a new way.

IV

The Message Of Mysticism

"We are saved by hope; but hope that is seen is not hope; for who hopeth for that which he seeth?" (Ro 8:24)

Mystical idealism is a constant in the cultural history of the Spanish people. It can be traced to the pre-Christian era of the deeply religious proto-Iberian culture, which produced what is called the *Devotio iberica*, a sacred oath of dedication of one's life to the lives of others. The bull was that culture's symbol of life and death: the *toro de lidia*[1] represented the struggle to the death between man and animal, the struggle through which, by displaying his willingness to make the ultimate sacrifice, a man became a warrior. In its origin this struggle to the death was religious in concept. It required the warrior to conquer his fear, man's greatest enemy, not out of vanity or pride or for economic gain but as symbol of the possibility that all men might live beyond fear even in the face of death. Perhaps it represented the mystic struggle, the conscious intentional suffering through which one may overcome the animal in the self. That process purifies the heart and raises man to a higher level of the self.

According to legend Christian mysticism began in Spain as far back as the first century when the Virgin Mary appeared to the apostle Saint James (who brought Christianity to Spain) on the banks of the Ebro:

---

1.   Lidia is derived from litigare, to fight.

[On 12 October of the year 39 James of Zebedeo was praying with his disciples on the banks of the Ebro. The night was dark. James had walked a short distance, when, suddenly, a shining light appeared. The mother of God appeared surrounded by thousands of angels. She was seated on a pillar of jasper. She was accompanied by Saint John the Evangelist. Some celestial voices intoned to the chords of a harp *la salve angélica*. The Virgin directed herself to James and told him: "Here I wish to be worshipped. Build me a temple and let this pillar remain in this place till the end of the world. Here I will work miracles." Obeying the orders of the most saintly Mary, James hurried to build a chapel, which was later called Our Lady of *Pilar*]. (López Ferreiro 1: 1139)

This event may well account for the fact that Spain was the first country in whose mystical development Mary occupied as significant a place as Jesus.

Fernando Rielo sees the universal church as sustained by four great branches or apostolic churches: the Johannine or symbolic church; the Pauline or philosophical church; the Petrine or juridical church; and the Jacobean or mystical church. Spain is the depository of the mystical church, as is confirmed by the emergence there of a powerful hermitical movement during the first four centuries A.D., a movement that spread through all of Latin Europe. This movement gave rise to a tradition of pilgrimages to Santiago (James) de Compostela, in Northern Spain. The hermitical movement was founded on the precept of worldly renunciation as a means of union with God (López Sevillano, "The Passage..." 2).

Spain's mystical theology acquired wide renown in early times through the teachings of San Isidoro, a Spaniard from Seville whose doctrine of *Sentencias* renewed mystical fervor. His thought consisted of three basic premises: first, that the soul, by virtue of its heavenly origin, might be betrothed to Christ; second, that purification is the only requisite for attaining this glorious state; and third, that "mystical union" is a mixing of the higher with the lower, both of which are one substance. San Isidoro's mystical teachings established the criteriological model that eventually projected itself into monasticism throughout Europe, including Ireland, France, and Italy (*Existe...* 139). His insistence that the "union of love" between the human and divine spirits calls for many sacrifices, for a practice of purifying asceticism, has led many writers to emphasize this practice as the fundamental feature of Spanish mysticism. For mysticism to be authentic in Rielo's view it must have the feature of asceticism; without it there is only pseudo-mysticism.

During the "Golden Age" of Spanish literature in the fifteenth and sixteenth centuries, the message of mysticism in Spain was refined and perfected through the work of three central figures: San Ignacio de Loyola, San Juan de la Cruz and Santa Teresa de Jesus. San Ignacio de Loyola was the founder of the "Company of Jesus"--a Jesuit order--and undoubtedly a model teacher for San Juan de la Cruz. In the spirit of the Crusades, San Ignacio dressed in armor in order to wage war for Christ (*San Ignacio*, Fontes 184-204). His mysticism, in contrast to that of San Juan or Santa Teresa, thus takes on the military character of an alliance with Christ Crucified and is couched in a rhetoric of strength and virility. San Ignacio calls man's higher faculties of feeling, understanding, and animation (life force) aspects of Divine essence, and explains this concept in the *Ejercicios espirituales* [*Spiritual Exercises*], the most famous of his teachings:

> ... God lives in creatures, in the elements that give being, in plants vegetating, in animals sensing, in men coming to understand, and thus in myself, giving me Being, animating, sensing, and making me understand; exactly in this way making a temple of me created in the likeness and image of his divine majesty. (*Ejercicios*, Fontes, 235)

According to San Ignacio, the attainment of divine union endows one with many "mystic gifts": consolation; tears; divine illuminations; intense love; tranquility of soul; infusions of faith, hope, and charity; and internal and external *Logüelas*, which are infused songs in the voice of the Divine Persons that reverberate within both the soul and the senses (258). He describes the mystic union as a communication of love:

> ... Love consists in communication of all the parts; it is a way for the lover, by giving what he has and communicating what he can, to know the beloved and thus, on the contrary, for the beloved to know the lover; so that if one has knowledge, one may give it to another who does not have it; if honors, if riches, the one who has may give to the one who lacks. (231)

Santa Teresa also links the experience of divine union, as exemplified by the mystical experiences of "heavenly visions" that she describes in her Autobiography, to the principle of giving, in this case to gifts left by the hand of God:

Like imperfect sleep which, instead of giving more strength to the head, doth but leave it the more exhausted, the result of mere operations of the imagination is but to weaken the soul. Instead of nourishment and energy she reaps only lassitude and disgust: whereas a genuine heavenly vision yields to her a harvest of ineffable spiritual riches, and an admirable renewal of bodily strength. I alleged these reasons to those who so often declared my visions the work of the enemy of mankind and the sport of my imagination.... I showed them the jewels which the divine hand had left with me: --they were my actual dispositions. All those who knew me saw that I was changed; my confessor bore witness to the fact; this improvement, palpable in all respects, far from being hidden, was brilliantly evident to all men. As for myself, it was impossible to believe that if the demon were its author, he could have used, in order to lose me and lead me to hell, an expedient so contrary to his own interest as that of uprooting my vices, and filling me with masculine courage and other virtues instead, for I saw clearly that a single one of these visions was enough to enrich me with all that wealth. ("Libro de la Vida" *Obras*... 137)

In the introduction to her *Las Moradas* [*The Rooms*] or *Castillo Interior* [*Interior Castle*], Tomás Navarro Tomás explains the fundamental metaphor through which Santa Teresa images the soul's union with God:

[She explains in it her doctrine, considering the soul as a magnificent castle, in whose center, in the richest and most secret room God is found. God is the supreme aspiration of mysticism. The incentive is love, and knowledge of oneself is the road; one arrives, then, to Him by going deep down in our spirit, studying our conscience, entering within ourselves to the bottom of this our interior castle; the Sainted Doctor of divine love guides the soul in said learning about oneself, and step by step leads from the fence of the castle to the last Room, in which waits the desired union with the Beloved.] (x-xi)

Perhaps the most important of the three Golden Age mystics for an understanding of Rielo, however, is San Juan de la Cruz, from whose work Rielo draws, but also transforms, some of the crucial tropes of his own poetry. One of these is "the dark night of the soul," a metaphor which San Juan uses to figure the three stages of faith that occur in the struggle for mystic union. The first stage is the "night" at the edge of sunset, in which faith darkens reason rather than illuminates it; the second stage is "night" in its darkest moment, when faith brings grave suffering in the soul and reason is so overcome that the only thing it understands is that it understands nothing. The third stage is the "night" at the edge of dawn, in which, moving beyond mere understanding, the soul *sees* the splendor of the Holy Trinity and apprehends the principle of humanity saved by Christ and raised to glory. In a poem titled "Clara noche oscura" ["Clear Dark Night"], Rielo both appropriates this metaphor and transforms it by making the "dark night" clear:

[How clear is the dark night
that even words awaken

in order not to pronounce themselves.

This awakening is not yet silence.
Silence is the rope with which the shout is hanged

because of this in the silence...

No one touches himself in order to see if he lives.]

Qué clara es la noche oscura
que hasta las palabras despiertan

para no pronunciarse.

Este despertar no es silencio todavía.
El silencio es la cuerda con que el grito se ahorca.

por eso en el silencio...

nadie se toca para ver si vive.

(*Noche clara* 101)

Rielo's "clear dark night" creates a sense of achieved union that is often missing in San Juan. Francisco Torres Marin, an *Idente* critic, asks in reference to Rielo's book *Noche clara,* in which the preceding poem appears: "Is it perhaps that in Rielo's life clarity defines night, in a daring existential pirouette that changes the sign of the concept of 'dark night' inherited from our classics?" (*Noche clara* 7). This indeed seems to be the case. For Rielo the mystic night is not dark, although it is defined by darkness. In a poem titled, "*Por fin, existo*" ["Finally I exist"], Rielo writes:

[Suffer not now the misfortune of bitter waves,
That, purified and full, to your clarity given
Like window that at last says:

Finally, I exist.]

Que ya no sufre el infortunio de olas amargas,
Que, depurada y plena, a tu claridad entrega
Como ventana que al fin se dice:

Por fin, existo.
(*Noche clara* 93)

Lack of God's "clarity" produces sleep, which Rielo describes poetically as:

[Loneliness that wanders errant like frustrated foam
through darkened rocks, not one lighted.
Thus is the life of so many creatures born
to love each other and, nevertheless, broken they live
like humiliating asphalt, destroyed.]

Soledad que errante vaga como frustrada espuma
por rocas apagadas, ninguna encendida.
Así es la vida de tantas criaturas nacidas
para amarse y, sin embargo, rotas viven
como asfalto humillante, destrozado.
("Balcón de amantes" ["Balcony of lovers"], 30)

Like San Ignacio and Santa Teresa, San Juan speaks directly of the "union of love" between God and man, though instead of Santa Teresa's metaphor of the castle he elaborates a desert landscape as the scene of this union where the soul:

[finds no terms, no means, no comparison that can express the sublimity of the wisdom and the delicacy of the spiritual feeling with which she is filled.... We receive this mystical knowledge of God clothed in none of the kinds of images, in none of the sensible representations, which our mind utilizes in other circumstances. Accordingly in this knowledge, since the senses and the imagination are not employed, we get neither form nor impression, nor can we give an account or furnish a likeness, although the mysterious and sweet-tasting wisdom comes home so clearly to the inmost parts of our soul. Imagine a man seeing a certain kind of thing for the first time in his life. He can understand it, use and enjoy it, but he cannot give a name to it, nor communicate any idea of it, even though all the while it is a simple thing of sense. How much greater will his powerlessness become when it goes beyond the senses! This is the peculiarity of the divine language. The more infused, intimate, spiritual, and supersensible it is, the more it exceeds the senses, both inner and outer, and imposes silence upon them.... The soul then feels as if placed in a vast profound solitude, to which no created thing has access, in an immense and boundless desert, desert the more delicious the more solitary it is. There, in this abyss of wisdom, the soul grows nourished by what it drinks from the well-springs of the comprehension of love... ("La noche oscura del alma" ["The Dark Night of the Soul"] *Vida y Obras.* Chp. 17, 3-6/ 675-676)

The vast solitude of the desert, where, according to San Juan, the soul's transformation takes place, is a symbol also used by many other mystics, including Rielo:

[Mysterious things happen in dreams
from those which later are born predictions.

I dreamed of flowers: none was certain.
There were no skies, not even tears.
Where the grief? where the touch?
All exiled in cosmos with destiny of none.

Suddenly, the desert.
And in me a sudden shock.

Only remains, Lord, death that endures.]

Suceden cosas misteriosas en sueños
de los que luego nacen predicciones.

Soñé con flores: ninguna era cierta.
No había cielos, ni aun lágrimas.
Dónde la pena? Dónde el tacto?
Todo exiliado en cosmos con destino de nadie.

De pronto, el desierto,
Y en mi un sobresalto.

Sólo queda, Señor, la muerte que subiste.
(*Balcón a la bahía* 35)

Although he draws upon several of San Juan's tropes, however, Rielo differs significantly from his precursor in the way he conceives of the presence of the divine in the human. San Juan delineates his conception of this presence when he writes: "... it is to be known that in all souls God dwells secretly and covered in their substance, because, if it were not so, they could not survive" (*Llama de amor viva*, Can. 4.14 (*Vida y Obras* 976)). San Juan still conceives of God as separate from human "substance," which is treated in the preceding sentence as a kind of outer skin or clothing, and this conception leads him to speak of "participation" in divine union. In his genetic metaphysics, Rielo, by contrast, elaborates a quite different concept of substance, a concept centered on unity that transcends any spirit-substance dichotomy and any attendant notion of "participation." Rielo calls matter "*congenitud*" ["congenuity"] and the "center" of this being "*deidad*" ["deity"], which is elevated in esoteric understanding to "*treidad*" ["threeness"]. According to this sacred law of three, the three forces of the absolute--Father, Son, and Holy Ghost--are manifested in everything including man. The higher mixes with the lower to activate the middle, thus making the lower higher and the higher lower. The law of Conscious Being is the true meaning of *treidad*; man's level of being is *related* through effort (aseticism) to that law, giving rise to a higher level of consciousness. *Treidad* is a symbol of the evolutionary process of

89

conscious work on Being, but its essence is the law of three itself. Rielo makes a comparison (which he precedes with a statement of the difficulty of any example) in the following words: *"treidad* is like a pyramid that, in relation to a beam of light, reverberates on all three faces." (*"Dos intérpretes..."* 9). *Treidad* is a sacred Law that is inherent in all levels of manifestation, and the understanding of this law and its conscious application to the self constitute the *mystic procession* that leads to union. Rielo establishes a strict difference between metaphysics and ontology within the Christian conception:

> [Metaphysics, science of the constitution of the absolute subject by the three divine persons, which being defined within themselves, are the absolute axiom; ontology, science of the constitution of the human being by constitutive presence in Him of the absolute subject. Metaphysics refers, therefore, in the strict sense of its deep meaning, *ad intra* to the absolute subject; ontology, also in the strict sense of its deep meaning, refers *ad extra* to the constitutive presence of the absolute act and the absolute subject in the human being. Mysticism is, in this sense, the genetic conception of ontology.] (*"Dos intérpretes..."* 9)

Thus we arrive at Rielo's definition of man, the logical conclusion of his genetic metaphysics: "human nature is essentially mystic." According to his mystic conception there is only one potential or faculty in man: the "potential of union" or "unitive faculty," of which the understanding and the will are only attributes. This conception separates him from San Juan de la Cruz and San Ignacio de Loyola, who base their concept of man on the Augustinian and Neoplatonic doctrine of the three potentials: understanding, memory and will.

This insistence on the fundamentally unitive nature of man also shapes Rielo's genetic conception of love, which he calls: *"transverberación divina"* [divine transverberation]. This conception denies the singularity of the absolute personal being, for it posits that at least two personal beings constitute one love, **essence**, or transverberation:

> The love of the Father cannot be expressed without the Son, the love of the Son cannot be expressed without the Father... In the field of reason love is *"binidad"* ("two-fold"), and in the revealed field, *"trinidad"* ("three-fold," or "trinity"). Mystic transverberation is love, a mutual understanding of the absolute subject and the

human being, in virtue of the constitutive presence of the former in the created element of the latter. ("*Dos intérpretes...*" 9)

Rielian mysticism is very much in tune with the esoteric Christianity found in modern writers outside Spain such as G.I. Gurdjieff[2]. For, like such writers, Rielo maintains that it is not enough to be "composed" or made up of the divine substance of God to attain a higher level of being, a higher consciousness, a developed soul. The "seed" must be planted, watered, cared for. *Desire*--the wish to *be*--must be strong in a man, and that man must make efforts to awaken. Rielo calls this effort "la mística procesión" ["the mystical procession"], describing this procession as "the elevation to the order of the supernatural of an ontological presence constitutive in its level of plenitude" (7). Gurdjieff calls this procession "Being-Partkdolg-duty": conscious labor and intentional suffering.

Rielo describes the mystic union as "communicative presence," a state of higher consciousness or sanctifying grace in which the human being is "Father with the Father, Son with the Son, and Holy Ghost with the Holy Ghost" (7). The symbol of Christ crucified and raised from the dead represents the transformation available to man if he "dies" to what he is and takes the teachings of Christ as "Third Force" and the Holy Ghost as the central moving force of existence. In order to "die" to what you are, "to enter into mystic union," according to San Juan, three forms of nothingness must be embraced: that of the senses, that of the powers, and that of substance. Thus, as Gurdjieff puts it, the total nothingness of the self is the starting point for the mystic experience (*All and Everything* n. pag.). Or, as Rielo writes in "Ciudad hallada," the soul must be unclothed:

[Take off your clothes
I cry to see you,
clean of mists
and your leaves you drop.]

¡Desnúdate!
Lloro por verte,

---

2. Founder of an ancient school called the Fourth Way that is still in existence in modern times as the Gurdjieff Foundation.

limpio de brumas...
y tus hojas dejes.

(Llanto azul 21)

In Rielo, as in Gurdjieff, the Law of Three is a cosmic, sacred law, a law that operates, in the form of affirming, denying, and neutralizing forces, in all manifestations of reality. Rielo calls this law the "*Santísima Trinidad*" ["Most Holy Trinity"], while Gurdjieff calls it "*Triamazikamno*" as pure-symbol.[3] Only in God are these three forces *one* and *inseparable*. The First and Second Force are always present and active in man, but the Third Force, the force necessary for conscious Being, is present only as potential or "seed." For ordinary, undeveloped man--man asleep, in esoteric terms--quotidian life or the external world constitutes the Third Force; it is only when man takes esoteric teachings, teachings like those of Christ or "the Fourth Way", as Third Force that a change of Being can take place. This change is the birth of a new man. It is the esoteric meaning of Christ's teaching that we must be "born of the spirit."

The entire volume *Paisaje desnudo* reveals the intimate interior landscape where "union" takes place when all the attributes of personality formed by life and the ego have been stripped away. The volume's first poem is titled "Ved" (the plural imperative form of the verb *to see*):

[I fly in night
that which in the day I cry.

See [*Ved*]

In the night I enclose
that which in the day I take
myyy...
Fingers

That's why my sleep I strum
with feather of a kiss.

---

3.   "Pure-symbol" in this context means a word that resists denotative definition and that must be understood purely contextually in the complexity of the complete ouevre.

Now isss. Do, re, mi...
a goodbye
a flight.

Love!

Come nights of love.
Come in dance of lights.
Come when I am awake.

Definitively
awake.

Awake...
and without me.]

Vuelo en noche.
lo que en el día lloro.

Ved.

En la noche encierro
lo que en el día tomo.
misss...
dedos

por eso mi sueño rasgueo
con pluma de un beso.

Ya essstá. Do, re, mi...
un adiós
un vuelo.

¡Amor!

Venid noches de amor.
Venid en danza de luceros.
Venid cuando esté despierto.

Definitivamente
despierto.

Despierto...
y sin mí.   (11)

This poem awakens into consciousness the inner vibrations of the words, emphasized by added letters that create vibrating sound in Spanish, and thus gives those words new power. A special light of attention is thus called forth by means of the intentional sensation invoked by every word and image beginning with "misss... dedos" ("myyy... fingers"). The line "Now isss. Do, re, mi...," followed immediately by "a goodbye / a flight," ties Rielo's thought inextricably to Gurdjieff's once again. The Law of Seven, symbolized graphically in Gurdjieff by the "enneagram," is symbolized also by the musical scale: Do, Re, Mi, Fa, Sol, La, Si, Do. It represents a cosmic law that functions in all manifestations of actions and relates to man in his search for conscious Being. The notes Do, Re, and Mi can be struck, but the Fa note--called "the bridge"--can only be sounded and thus "crossed" by means of a conscious shock of *self*-remembering and sensing the whole of oneself here and now. Thereby one keeps one's actions in line with the aim of one's intentional direction. Rielo's "flight" after striking the note *Mi,* which finally ends in awakening, marks the crossing of the *Fa* bridge of the "enneagram."

Another point of contact between Rielo and Gurdjieff lies in a common question fundamental to the works of both: *who am I*? This question, posed seriously, calls forth investigation, pondering, and self-observation. Rielo's version of this question appears in a poem titled "Se nace de la noche" ["It is born of the night"]:

[Who am I? What do I love? Do I think perhaps?]

¿Quién soy? ¿Qué amo? ¿Pienso acaso?
(*Noche clara* 94)

For both Rielo and Gurdjieff this question is a necessary step in the process by which man may awaken from his hypnotized state to a state of conscious Being and activate the higher powers in himself.

Although comparisons between Rielo and the Spanish Golden Age mystics or Gurdjieff illuminate some of the crucial elements of

94

Rielo's mysticism, what remains to be carried out (a project that most studies of modern mystic poetry simply fail to take up) is a practical analysis of the meaning behind the mystic states of the poet. What does it mean to have one's soul united with God? What actually occurs in the person who experiences this consummation? How is he changed, and what in him changes? The scriptures define this change in its incommensurable aspect: "The wind blows where it lists, and you hear its voice but do not know whence it comes and whither it goes; so is every one that is born of the spirit" (John 3:8). This esoteric Christian teaching speaks of another kind of man, a completely new man. The new man is "born of the spirit" and thus enters into a state where quotidian concerns no longer define the axis of existence. Having achieved a higher level of consciousness, he gains for the first time the capacity to "hear" the extraordinary understandings that issue from higher centers within. As Paul puts it, "Now we know in part, but then shall I know fully, even as also I have been fully known" (Co. 13:22). In the new man the powerful emotion of self-love and the limited logic of yes *or* no rule no longer; thought based only on the evidence of the external world and its senses is seen for what it is: the shut, unbalanced thinking of those who still grope in darkness.

Rielo's writing and voice thus found themselves on the idea of the higher possibilities of mankind, of mankind as a creation with a "divine spark" or potentiating seed of self-development in the inner realm of his consciousness and spirit. Conceiving of God not as located in the visible world of space and time but as uncreate, as spirit, as an order of truth, Rielo uses his themes and forms not to create outward reflections of that visibile world, but rather to create inward reflections of invisible, untouchable realities. His life and works are in accordance with the saying of Christ: "God is Spirit: and they that worship him must worship in Spirit and in Truth" (John 4:24). As Rielo writes:

[Time only of Cross, that falls at times
from my shoulders tired by unconsciousness
Eternal Cireneo[4], you give it back to me
to arrive at your open hands.

---

4.   Cireneo was the man who carried the cross of Jesus after he fell and could no longer carry it.

95

Tell me if the Golgotha that now does not wound
only astonishes he who lover comes arriving
from a death that never was his death,
but yours on cross, my beloved Christ.

You, with your unique being, star of mine,
absolute truth that I desire
without possible rest on my path,

The griefs of my life you glorify
as much as the love with which I love you
without world or heaven to stop it.]

Tiempo sólo de cruz, que cae a veces
de mis hombros cansados por desmayo,
Eterno Cireneo, me la devuelves
para llegar a tus abiertas manos.

Dime si el Gólgota que ya no hiere
sólo asombra al que amante va llegando
de una muerte que nunca fue su muerte,
sino la tuya en cruz, mi Cristo amado.

Tú, con tu sola estancia, estrella mía,
absoluta verdad que yo deseo
sin posible descanso en mi vereda,

Las penas de mi vida glorificas
tanto como el amor con que te quiero
sin que mundo ni cielo lo interfiera.

(Dolor entre cristales 23)

The message of mysticism is a plea for seeing the reality of
ourselves and the world we have built. We cannot deny the fact that
we are violent and jealous, that we are in continual conflict; much of
our lives seems like a battlefield where there is little serenity, little
understanding, and little love, except for self-love. The message of
Rielo's mystical poetry is that there is another possibility; there *is* a way
to live free from violence, envy, hate, and jealousy--free from the
confining prison walls of self-interest and self-love. Freedom *is*
possible. But in order to change the world one must first change

oneself: one must transform one's being, acquire a higher state of consciousness. The lower, animalistic state of consciousness, the animal, must be quieted or dissolved through awareness, understanding, and contemplation, making space for the higher-emotional and higher-intellectual centers, which are already prepared to function. Although shrouded in mystery and often buried in difficult texts by religious or mystic writers, these ideas have been stated again and again throughout the ages.

The message of mystic union is the direct cognition that all things originate from God and end with God. All the laws of the universe are one. This unity of all creation cannot be comprehended in the ordinary state of consciousness. It is an experience of a higher state of being, a higher level of consciousness. The ordinary level of consciousness is "caught" in the outer world of appearances, of that which can be known with the senses. At this ordinary level of ones being, the inner self, the essence or soul, is undeveloped and its powers are absent, or "asleep," as esoteric Christianity puts it. When attention and awareness are turned inward, and discursive thought is replaced by physical or bodily awareness, active attention, and silent presence, then the soul or "real I" (Gurdjieff) has space to awaken and develop. One's part in the whole of time and space is felt and lived.

Like Jacob Boehme, who turned to the Bible for help when he felt unable to express his experiences in words, Rielo draws heavily upon the parabolic language of the Bible in many of his poems in order to articulate his mystic message. This language serves both as a springboard and a guide to the reader. Rielo's parables themselves center thematically on the hidden nature of man. A poem from *Dolor entre Cristales*, for example, is introduced by the parable of the mustard seed and the kingdom of heaven, which has been explained by other esoteric writers as the "doctrine of potentiality":

> The Kingdom of heaven is like unto a grain of mustard seed, which a man took, and sowed in his field: Which indeed is the least of all seeds: but when it is grown, it is the greatest among herbs, and becometh a tree, so that the birds of the air come and lodge in the branches thereof. (Mt. 13:31-33)

In this parable, the seed is likened to the kingdom of heaven, where the tiniest of seeds grows into a towering tree larger than any other in the garden, a tree where even birds can nest. This analogy reveals the enormous difference between man's ordinary state and the "kingdom of heaven" which is "within man." The ordinary man is incomplete, but he carries within himself the potential of reaching higher states of being and consciousness. He can develop into a being of very different qualities and powers. In Gurdjieff's teachings man's ordinary state is compared to being asleep in bed, while the achieved state of higher consciousness is compared to the waking state in which one walks, eats, and speaks. The idea of such a tremendous difference is staggering. What would we be like if this potentiality were fulfilled? In esoteric Christianity it is taught that Christ embodies this transformation: "I am the way and the truth and the life, no one goes to the Father but by me" (John 14:6). And what is He like? His essence is love. He is the embodiment of a world without violence, brutality, envy, pride, or self-interest; his vision is an integrated world of man, nature, and God.

By introducing his poem with the parable of the mustard seed, Rielo stretches a double cord of attention for the reader: a feeling of the whole of oneself and a simultaneous, objective, impartial observation of external phenomena. His purpose is the revelation of the nature of the "Kingdom of Heaven," and his method in the poem itself consists in a lyric re-creation of the parable:

[Having arrived at the Medical Center
of New York University,
I contemplate one more time the corpulent trees:
the color of their leaves cannot be described
by pathetic hand: this vertical beauty
conquers the modesty of the poet.
Only the dazzling silence could perhaps recreate it.
The destitute leaves fall to the dull feet of earth:
to step on them is to step on my own death
and to await new spring in which to be born again each day
is law of human existence in transit to happy destiny
from which now there is no return to pilgrim sob.
Eternal spring where nothing perishes!

None of the trees is like that of the mustard
that Christ elevates to symbol as kingdom of Heaven
born this tree of the smallest seed,
the birds that in its leaves nest are souls, just flight
that in pure contemplation repose.
Man is bird, that unique, does not die

in leaves illuminated by spilled cross blood:
his breath is everlasting landmark
of a mustard, indivisible breeze, so far from death.

Tree by love redeemed
husband of a flesh that in its pact
man ceases to be sad
because winter does not exist that its branches unleaf

Oh rapture of blood converted into bloodless wine
by a heaven populated with its mystic forest.]

Llegado al hospital Medical Center
de la universidad de Nueva York,
contemplo una vez más los corpulentos árboles:
el color de sus hojas no puede ser descrito
por patética mano: esta hermosura vertical
vence el pudor del poeta.
Sólo el silencio deslumbrante podría acaso recrearla.
Las hojas desvalidas caen a los pies opacos de la tierra:
Pisarlas es pisar mi propia muerte
y esperar nueva primavera en que nacer de nuevo cada día
es ley de una existencia humana en tránsito a feliz destino
del que ya no se vuelve al peregrino llanto.
¡Eterna primavera donde nada perece!

Ninguno de los árboles es como el de mostaza
que Cristo eleva a símbolo del Reino de los Cielos.
Nacido este árbol de la semilla más pequeña,
las aves que en su fronda anidan son justo vuelo de almas
que en la contemplación pura reposan.
El hombre es ave que, única, no muere
en fronda iluminada por sangre en cruz vertida:
su hálito es hito perdurable
de una mostaza, brisa indivisible, cuán lejos de la muerte.

Arbol por el amor redento
esposo de una carne que en su pacto
el hombre deja de ser triste
porque no existe invierno que sus ramas deshoje.

¡Oh rapto de la sangre convertida en incruento vino
por un cielo poblado con su místico bosque!
(Dolor entre cristales 21-22)

Not even the sublime beauty of the eternal spring, nor the promise
of a happy destiny can be as glorious as the mustard seed, the symbol
of the Kingdom of Heaven, the transformation of being. In this poem,
published in 1990, we see that Rielo's symbolism is consistent through
his entire poetic creation. In his first volume of verse *Dios y árbol*,
published in 1958, "tree" is the symbol of man, just as it is in the beautiful
poem just quoted. The mustard tree is the pure-symbol of the idea of
the potentiality and the possibility of man's psychological evolution, an
evolution not automatic as in nature, but self-developed through effort
and the wish to *be*. This pure-symbol is further defined by its continual
flux and change within the context of the poem's structure. Therefore,
it cannot be "defined" as such. Any definable ready-made symbol is
simply pseudo-symbol. The only permanent characteristic of Rielo's
pure-symbolism, and of the pure-symbol in general, is its parallelism
with nature in all the richness of its infinite possibilities and potential
meanings. These meanings flow and change throughout the poem by
congenesis, to use a rielian term, they nonetheless remain the same. An
apt metaphor through which to figure pure-symbolism might be the
flowing of a river: it is ever changing, and yet always the same. One can
"read" the river on many different levels also. The simplest mind and
the most highly developed will each understand it, feel communication
with it, and learn from it in his own way, even if only aesthetically. This
openness to multiple but congenitive readings confirms the
extraordinary importance of Rielo in the mystical tradition. In the past
mystic poetry was relegated to initiates, to the few who possessed
"secret" knowledge. Rielo brings these dark secrets to the light of day.
He maintains that the time has come for all hidden knowledge to be
brought within the grasp of every man. Rielo's pure-symbolism offers
readers key words and phrases that open mystical ideas to a variety of
levels of interpretation, as well as setting those ideas in the context of
very familiar higher literature such as the Bible. The emotional quality
of Rielo's lyricism allows the pure-symbol to "speak" to the other mind
of the heart. The musical, rhythmic quality, of his poetry also
communicates by means of little-studied human responses not related
to thought and reason.

In a poem published in 1989, Rielo uses pure-symbolism to speak
directly of the unconscious condition of ordinary man:

100

[What spring opening me swift road
between rays of sun
or grains in torrents of life.

It had no consciousness: this is world of shadows.
I sprang from light to light in multitude of birds.
Enthusiasm was the air of my name.

When the innocent hour is called forth.
When life smells new born.
When the unbreakable brilliance wounds...
arises the sad virgin sob of desire.

Not in niche of paining flesh.
Not in consciousness of day to day history.
Not in order to live again with window to heaven.

Space of my familiar dreams
I wait for you... in this ruby silver
of my sunset and its open hand!]

Qué primavera abriéndome veloz camino
entre rayos de sol
o mieses en torrentes de vida.

No tenía conciencia: ésta es mundo de sombras.
Yo saltaba de luz en luz con multitud de pájaros.
Entusiasmo era el aire de mi nombre.

Cuando se evoca la inocente hora.
Cuando la vida huele a recién hecha.
Cuando el fulgor inquebrantable hiere...
surge el llanto triste virgen del deseo.

No en nicho de doliente carne.
No en conciencia de historia cotidiana.
No para volver a vivir con ventana al cielo.
¡Espacio de mis sueños familiares
te espero... en este rosicler
de mi ocaso y su abierta mano!

(*Balcón a la bahía* 27)

101

In this poem, the esoteric teaching of the necessity of detachment from desire and the world of senses, a teaching found in the *Upanishads* and other Eastern spiritual writings, is expressed by Rielo in a strikingly original and lyrical symbol: "El llanto triste virgen del deseo" ["The sad virgin sob of desire"]. Pure-symbol such as this is the highest form of teaching available to writers, since it is the densest carrier of meaning. Several profound ideas are layered together, so to speak, in a single concise brush stroke of words. In ancient times masters and initiates of esoteric knowledge used similar techniques to guard their "secrets" so that higher ideas did not become distorted by ordinary understanding and were not put to improper purposes. As the Scriptures put it, "Pearls are not cast before swine, lest they turn and rend you" (Mt 7:6). Rielo, however, uses pure-symbol to offer his reader a pure *impression*, paradoxically revealed and withheld simultaneously, of a higher conscious order, of the inner circle of humanity.

In the central pure-symbol of the preceding poem, "desire" is "virgin," untouched by man, chaste, not "known" by man. In other words, desire for objects of the external world is forfeited. The words "llanto triste" ["sad sob"] further densify this symbol by revealing the intentional suffering and struggle necessary for detachment from desire and the death of personality to take place. It is revealed in empirical mysticism that suffering is absolutely necessary, that it stands in accordance with the two sacred, cosmic laws. Without suffering no transformation, no change of being, can take place. If one does not experience this suffering, one must seek it out. This spiritual law might be parallel to the physiological law that makes the suffering of exercise (the overcoming of inertia) necessary in order to develop a muscle. This idea is clarified by the line: "No tenía conciencia: ésta es mundo de sombras" ("It was not conscious: this is a world of shadows"). The meaning is explicit: there is no consciousness. The world is a world of shadows and the darkness of sleep. The mystic message, however, may call forth the experience of change in conscious being: the experience of higher states of consciousness and the beginning of the functioning of higher-intellectual and higher-emotional centers (P.D. Ouspensky, *The Fourth Way* 5).

In this poem "light" is the pure-symbol of consciousness and is described as scattered or multiple, perhaps distributed into a range of degrees or levels: "yo saltaba de luz en luz con multitud de pájaros" ["I jumped from light to light in multitud of birds"]. The verb *saltar* ["to

jump"] in this sentence is cast in the imperfect past tense: "saltaba."
This tense, which we do not have in English and for which therefore no exact translation is possible, expresses the idea of action ongoing in the past; of habitual, repeated action; of a process of continued movement. Cast in this tense, the trope of jumping symbolizes the effort continually required in order to sustain higher levels of consciousness. One can never sustain such consciousness automatically, without effort; one must continually bring to life one's attention, awareness, and sensations. Through the phrase "con multitud de pájaros" ["in multitude of birds"], Rielo further densifies the pure-symbol of the jump by visualizing lyrically for the reader the rush of movement, the freedom of ascent to new heights. This "multitude of birds" flies with the wings of freedom, lifting man from the dark shadows of a sleeping unconscious world to the light of apprehension of a higher state of the self. It brings to the pure-symbol of which it constitutes an elemental part the connotation of freedom from the chains of sleep, conditioning, anger, and violence that mark man's ordinary state.

The poetic "I" in this poem is waiting for "*¡Espacio!*" ["Space!"].
The "sad virgin sob of desire" flows not into flesh, nor into quotidian-historical life, nor even into a life with windows to Heaven. Rather, it flows into "space," which was previously occupied by familiar dreams: the ordinary state of consciousness in undeveloped man. This "space" takes in the whole of the self in the eternal now, with its sunset an open hand of transformed being. It becomes the locus of a mystic union with the essence of the God, with the Absolute.

It is important to note that the suffering which must be undergone in order to transform one's being ultimately does not affect the soul itself. In the mystic state, one experiences or perceives pain, cruelty, and violence as an observer: such suffering is not allowed to touch the core of one's being. What suffers or feels pain is only the self-image built by ordinary, mechanical, sleeping man through tradition, education, and culture. For that image--an image figured by conscious being as the "animal"--must be overcome through the understanding, awareness, and effort that generate freedom. In another poem from *Balcón a la bahía*, we read:

[Higher still than ideas of the world:
                    the astonishing moment.

103

Ideas are clouds: mixture of light and shadow,
        small indecisive bodies

I have seen them crackle like paper
in definitive fire, be put out.
        Now I see what I do not see!]

Más alto que las ideas del mundo:
        el instante asombroso.

Las ideas son nubes: mezcla de luz y sombra
        pequeños cuerpos indecisos.

Las he visto crujir como papel
en fuego definitivo, extinguirse.
        ¡Ahora veo lo que no veo!   (40)

"The astonishing moment" is a pure-symbol of the present moment in conscious being, of the *presence* which transcends all thought, all the ideas of the world. Ideas are not elemental and thus hardly real; they are only composite bodies, mixtures of light and shadow. As they are extinguished, the poet reaches a new and higher level where new powers are experienced as real: "*Ahora veo lo que no veo!*" ["Now I see what I do not see!"]. There are now two men, one within the other: the seeing spirit has been born.

In yet another poem from the same volume Rielo re-affirms the insufficiency of this-worldly knowledge:

[How much science in my perch.
It reminds me that I am only passing through
        like the river.

My perch is like ancient oak
That incites my memory:
        within this, life.

How my destiny embraces it.
How its *presence* is perpetuated.]

Cuánta ciencia en mi percha.
Me recuerda que estoy de paso
   como el río.

Mi percha es como anciano roble
que incita mi memoria:
   dentro de ésta, la vida.

Cómo la abraza mi destino.
Cómo se perpetúa su presencia.   (43)

Like the works of the classical Spanish mystics, this poem turns to the interior path, to the depths of the self, to the pure essence of being. Science and memory are only reminders of death, of the rapid passing of the body. And both the body and its quotidian desires and forms of knowledge are undone by the other world within, where life is embraced by destiny, where life's *presence* is perpetuated.

Rielo's mysticism draws heavily on ideas that were fundamental to the thinking of pre-modern eras. One of these is the concept of levels, or scale. This concept remained very much alive as recently as in the Renaissance, but it seems foreign to scientific modes of thought that depend upon the evidence of the senses and thereby create the appearance that everything can be placed on the same scale. For that reason, it is commonly overlooked and is relegated to the thought of mystics and spiritual leaders, in spite of its potential for ordering a chaotic and violent world. A second pre-modern idea fundamental to both Rielo's genetic metaphysics and his poetry is that of man as created from and therefore a part of a vast living universe: man *in* and *of* the world. This idea seems to have lost much of its power in the modern, materialistic world where we seek sensual, tangible proof for everything, where we see man as separate from the world and often as master of the world. The material, sensual world has taken precedence over the world of idea and spirit. The Platonic notion that behind the visible phenomenal world lies another, invisible one of a greater order of reality has faded for most; but it has not faded for Rielo. He makes this point very clearly in a poem called "Clear Day":

[She, with her time, lost in wings
intimate and brief, my sigh, fleshless flight,
gives back to the nest; the nest, that before the world was,
I, pure idea, always inhabited.]

105

Ella, con su tiempo, perdido en alas,
íntimo y breve, mi suspiro, vuelo sin carne,
al nido devuelve; al nido, que, antes que el mundo fuere,
yo, pura idea, lo habitara siempre.

(Llanto azul 78)

Our material world of the senses is only a limited projection of the real world that lies beyond it, the reality on a higher scale that can only be experienced through a change in oneself, a change in one's own level of consciousness, one's state of being. The activity of the mind, body, and feelings, once released from that ordinary consciousness which is caught outside itself in the material world, allows a consciousness of a totally different nature to function. This phenomenon cannot be witnessed or experienced from the perspective of the lower state of consciousness.

In *Llanto azul*, Rielo describes an experience of this transformed consciousness, of this conscious Being:

[I am before you, birds.
I am before you, breezes.
I am before you, immutable blue, in the reason of existence.
I am before you in blues bathed
the star that in my heart complains.]

Yo soy antes que vosotras, aves.
Yo soy antes que vosotras, brisas.
Yo soy antes que tú, azul inmutable, en la razón de existir.
Yo soy antes que tú en azules bañaras
la estrella que en mi corazón se queja.

(Llanto Azul 78)

He compares this state to rest or repose in eternity:

[...as a naked virgin,
who hasn't even universes,
in her bridal bed rests
        always
        the same.]

... que como desnuda virgen,
que ni universos tiene,
en su tálamo descansa
    siempre
    la misma.
       (*Llanto azul* 78)

The image of the bridal bed is reminiscent of the imagery found in the *Song of Songs* and the poetry of San Juan and Santa Teresa. The metaphor of the naked virgin in her bridal bed resting defines that form of repose in which the soul awaits the active force, her husband. In this repose the soul awaits the creative act that will bring to the world of man new life, a new beginning, a new possibility. Rielo's position is clear: this state is beyond thought and beyond ordinary reason:

[... place never touched,
so blue ... that it seems abstract,
its passion teaches that crying is useless
for whoever was born to polish blues
in tireless spheres that the mind conquers.]

... lugar nunca tocado,
tan azul ... que parece abstracto,
su pasión enseñe que llorar es inútil
a quien naciera para pulir azules
en esferas incansables que la mente conquiste.   (81)

It is a state where things of the earth, of the material world, are not the focus:

[Leave also the earth, the earth is good
for dead clay jars.]

Deja también la tierra. La tierra basta
para tinajas muertas.   (81)

This state demands to be articulated in simple, emotional, and communicative images, as the following short poem--"No es rosa" ["It Is Not Rose"]--makes clear:

107

[It is not Rose...
        It is not water...

It is your soul sweetalive
        in things...]

No es rosa...
        No es agua...

Es tu alma dulceviva
        en las cosas...
            (*Dios y árbol* 23)

    Incommunicability has been called the keynote of mystical truth because such truth is not discursive but intuitive. It has been said that only ecstasy and transformation of being and consciousness can reveal esoteric knowledge, which is therefore considered extremely difficult of access and sometimes dismissed as mere "imagination" or "nonsense." The lyrical aspect of poetry, however, with its tremendous emotional appeal, strikes a cord in the reader that reason cannot strike. Perhaps that is why the *Idente* scholars call the mystical life "poetry."

    Metamorphic transformations of natural images often serve in Rielo's verse as pure-symbols for change of Being, for the process by which one enters into mystic life. In a poem from *Dios y árbol* titled "Apresar el verso" ["Capture the verse"], we read:

        [To sieze the verse
        that with the water runs...

Broken always in tears,
        evaporated by the air...

And he that comes...
        now is other.]

        Apresar el verso
        que con el agua corre...

108

Roto siempre en lágrimas,
                con el aire se evapora...

Y el que viene...
                ya es otro.   (29)

Perhaps Rielo's clearest articulations of mystical union, however,
are sounded in those poems in which God is presented as speaking to
the poet:

[Destiny is throat for the highest of songs
of someone as free as amethyst
of a kiss that is its nakedness.
In this way... the laws of a kiss
say it all or say nothing.

You have, son, happy vocation
not required to appeal to death
in order to understand as lover the mystery of life.
It is enough that you sing in your sleepless dreams
when asleep, son, you feel yourself celestial.

If you are awake, smile. I do not permit
you to cry... because it denies that I exist.
Don't you know that you do not belong to such
and that they have never been mine?
They are for those that have no greater destiny
than to live for themselves like color that flees
from a breast that they never found.

You I have loved, son, you I have loved.
When you almost did it with thought sob.
Then to your newly born consciousness
I brought myself and with the most chaste of breezes
from brilliant gardens I caressed you warm,
so you seemed bathed in the blood
of a warm afternoon, prodigal in gold walkers.

You, Son have been sweet presence
of my eternal happy days, virgin idea,
of you being first born on an earth
that you were never to live in your heart

but rather in mine. Not even its light
could enter you in unthinkable shadows.

I confirm to you that the hour that presides over
my happiness always will be yours, yours.
Yours, like naked landscape retained
that never slips on intranquil lawn.
Nor will I make ascentions that are not with you.
Nor will I any longer think worlds that you don't know
although they don't exist; you will be, yes, yes, he who puts
new wings on the birds so that your name
in its flight be evident far beyond the zenith of the world.
Yes. Sealed in love, you will be with me...
                      that which eternal I sigh.]

Destino es garganta para canto altísimo
de alguien tan libre como amatista
de un beso que lo es desnudo.
Por eso... las leyes de un beso
lo dicen todo o nada dicen.

Tú tienes, hijo, vocación dichosa
que no tiene que apelar a la muerte
para entender amante el misterio de la vida.
Basta que cantes en tus sueños insomnes
cuando dormido, hijo, te sientas celeste.

Que si despierto, sonríe. No permito
que llores... porque nieguen que existo.
¿No sabes que tú no eres de ellos
ni ellos míos han sido nunca?
Son ellos que no tienen mayor destino
que sólo vivirse como color que huye
de un pecho que nunca encontraron.

A ti te he amado, hijo, a ti te he amado.
Cuando tú casi lo hacías con pensado llanto.
Entonces a tu conciencia recién estrenada
yo me llegaba y con brisas castísimas
de jardines fúlgidos te acariciaba cálido,

que tú parecías como bañado en sangre
de una tarde pródiga en caminantes oros.

Tú, hijo, has sido dulce presencia
en mis eternos alegres días, virgen idea,
de ser tú primigenio en una tierra
que nunca habrías de vivir en tu pecho
más que en el mío. Ni siquiera su luz
podría entrarte en sombras impensables.

Yo te confirmo que la hora que preside
mi dicha siempre será tuya, tuya.
Tuya como desnudo paisaje retenido
que nunca resbala en césped intranquilo.
Ni haré ascenciones que no sea contigo.
Ni pensaré ya mundos que tú no conozcas
aunque no existan; serás, sí, sí, quien ponga
a las aves alas nuevas para que tu nombre
en su vuelo conste más allá del cenit del mundo.
Sí. Sellado en el amor, serás conmigo...
                    lo que eterno suspiro.
        ("Vocación" ["Vocation"], *Noche clara* 31)

This poem begins with freedom, the aim of awakening: "Free as an
amethyst / of a kiss that is its nakedness." The polychromatic pictorial
imagery is color beyond form, touched with the mystic aura of a "kiss."
Amethysts are purple crystals that vary from a timid grey orchid color,
to a rose-purple, and finally to a strong reddish purple. Traditional
mythical qualities attributed to amethysts include loyalty in the wearer
and healing powers. In the next lines, however, we learn that freedom
is attended by laws--"the laws of a kiss"--that originate at a level above
the planets. Help is available from this level when action is in
accordance with these laws. In the next verse, God speaks to the poet
of immortality attained by means of conscious love: the mystery of life.
The sacred force of sensation is included in the line "you feel yourself
celestial." The third verse touches on awakening and the total
elimination of negative emotions: God says, "I do not permit you to cry."
In order to expose the obstacles posed by negativity, this verse proceeds
to images depicting those who do not make efforts to stave off the
constant pressure of sleep. Such individuals are also compared to
colors that do not follow the laws of their origin or essence. As this
comparison suggests, such individuals do not engage in conscious

effort. They live only for themselves and do not attain either a high destiny in life or immortality at a higher level beyond death: ["they ... have no greater destiny / than to live for themselves, like colors that flee / from the breast they have never found."] In the fourth verse "presencia" ["presence"] is the key word. The poet's body on earth was formed in a sacred way; one of its functions is to receive forces directly from God, forces which make the poet, symbol of all men, conscious and free. The "sob that is thought" of the previous verse symbolizes the "lightgiving" force of attention in the feeling center--the force that gives the poet the power to awaken. Finally, the last verse contains God's promise of eternal joy and eternal life: ["...far beyond the zenith of the world. / Yes. Sealed in love you will be with me...."]

Immanuel Kant, a philosopher much admired by Rielo, concluded that we structure the physical world through the workings of the mind, which, with its own innate qualities, arranges and organizes the flow of incoming sensation. The mind itself re-creates the outer world by endowing it with some quality beyond those of the "thing-in-itself." Both the Indian philosophical idea of "*maya*" and Rielo's genetic metaphysics present a similar conclusion: our perception of the world and reality is limited by the narrowness of the senses. This conclusion can be confirmed by examining the known facts of science. The eyes "see" because of vibrations of light which, seen as a whole, is white, but which, split via a prism, is revealed as the seven colors of the spectrum. The vibration of a violet color is twice as rapid as that of the red at the opposite end of the scale. In other words, we do not see what really *is*, but only what we are conditioned to see by the limits of our organs of perception and our language. True understanding of the limits of the senses is an idea of transforming power, an idea central to Rielo's philosophy and poetry.

The American philosopher William James expands upon this idea when, discussing states that transcend the ordinary limits of the sense, he writes: "our normal waking consciousness, rational consciousness, is but one special type of consciousness, while all about it, parted from it by the flimsiest of screens, there are potential forms of consciousness entirety different" (97). Etymologically, the term "consciousness" means "knowing-together." A higher state of consciousness would therefore mean an expansion of this "knowing-together," an expansion which which would necessarily change the man or woman who experiences it. This change is so total that it is expressed by the

112

traditional mystics and Rielo as *dying*. One must die to what one was before in order to be re-born into conscious Being.

The mystic experience, then, is an experience of conscious being, an experience which opens the understanding of one's cosmic role. This experience encompasses and penetrates the whole of one's being so that all levels within are understood simultaneously: the mind, the body, the feelings, the instincts and cosmic laws. And that understanding, as the image of ["a blood that touching sets its beat inflame"] as the following passage affirms, becomes the transformed individual's *raison d'être*:

[This consciousness ends in Someone eternal
that key in hand gives me birth into new life.

Something extinguishes the mystery of the night
to be new, unusual, birth.
This you are, dreamed death: key of passage
to a blood that touching sets its beat inflame.]

Esta conciencia acaba en Alguien eterno
que llave en mano me nace a nueva luz.

Algo extingue el misterio de la noche
para ser nuevo, insólito, nacimiento.
Esto eres, muerte en sueño: llave de paso
a una sangre que tocando enciendo su pálpito.
(*Balcón a la bahía* 56)

The transformation figured here through tropes of re-birth and pulsing blood re-appears in the simple poem "Despiertame" ["Awaken Me"] in the form of the pure-symbol of awakening. To be awakened, this poem suggests, is the poet's true calling; the poet listens "with [his] wings together as if in prayer":

[Awaken me, ah, with your music
of always.

With that music
that says:

113

Listen, son, the birth
of your near destiny.

Destiny which I listen to
with my wings together.]

Despiértame, ay, con tu música
de siempre.

Con esa música
que dice:
Escucha, hijo, la partitura
de tu pronto destino.

Destino que escucho
con mis alas juntas.

(Dios y árbol 92)

"Awakening" is man's destiny: that is the message of mysticism; that
is God's message of harmony within sacred laws of Being.

V

Symbolism:
The Mystical Language Of Consciousness

"In the beginning was the Word, and the Word *was* with God, and the Word *was* God."   (John 1:1)

Fernando Rielo, as I have already noted, is a theoretician of poetry as well as a poet. In his masterpiece of literary criticism, *Teoría del Quijote: Su mística hispánica*; [*Theory of Don Quijote: Its Hispanic Mysticism*] he discusses the concept of "pure poetry," a concept fundamental to any understanding of the workings of the symbolic language that lies at the heart of Rielo's own poetic practice:

> As regards essential poetry, French lyricists during the 19th and 20th centuries have attempted to discover it, starting with Baudelaire ... in his pure synesthesia; Mallarmé, in pure absence; Laforgue, in pure enigma; Valery, in pure words.... The essence of the poetic function has not been clearly defined... thus Martinet speaks of "grades of redundancy", Foucault of "radical intransitiveness," Jacobson of "trans-rationality," Ferraté of "ambiguity," Barthes of "secondary super-significance", Tinjanov of "dynamitization" and "de-automatization," Shklovsky of "defamiliarization," and Belyi, Blok and Ivanov of "metaphysics" all in relation to the poetic word. (69-71)

In contrast to these theories, Rielo's personal theory and definition of pure poetry emphasizes transformation:

> Poetic function is derived from the behavior of the general law of art: the transformative function (not quite in the manner of critical

generativists as alternative facts of linguistic violation), which reduces to zero the specifics of linguistic function, thus constituting the manifestations of language within the infrastructure taken over by aesthetics.

("Theory of Don Quijote" 71)

Thus pure poetry, in Rielo's definition, is a function not of linguistics but of transformational aesthetics. Symbolism in Rielo's poetry reveals this transformative function: words have symbolic significance derived from an authority higher than the poet himself and can thus carry the power of transformational ideas. Symbolism becomes a universal language where the highest truths are expressed by means of figures or thought-forms projected simultaneously onto more than one level of reference. This theory sets the stage for an analysis of symbolism as the mystical language of consciousness.

Rielo uses the language of symbols to express esoteric, metaphysical content in his mystical poetry. The single word that most closely approximates a   description of his system of symbolism is "quintessence," defined in *Webster's* as:

1. The fifth essence, or ultimate substance of which heavenly bodies were thought to be composed in ancient and medieval philosophy: distinguished from the four elements air, fire, water, and earth;

2. The pure concentrated essence of anything;

3. The most perfect manifestation or embodiment of a quality or thing.

Rielo uses pure-symbol in his poetry as a spiritual language that transcends the particularity of one time and one place, that articulates "quintessential" spiritual realities. His pure-symbols reflect consistently the metaphysical concern for the "soul of souls" revealed as unity, multiplicity, and non-duality. In mystic poetry words reveal meaning simultaneously on more than one level depending on the context in which they are used and the manner in which they are inter-woven and embroidered. For this reason, a pure-symbol can never be precisely defined. To be pure, a symbol must remain open to the continual movement of thought, feelings, and understanding, to the constant flux of change both in the vertical dimension of the noumenal world of the spirit and eternity and in the horizontal dimension of the phenomenological world of time, space and matter. The symbol that can be precisely defined is a pseudo-symbol and cannot be called creative art. In contrast to subjective art, which is centered in the expression of the self and its desires, thoughts, and feelings, Rielo's symbolism transcends the "confusion of tongues" by the creation of a universal language of objective art in which the object is presented in its relationship to what it is part of, and to what is part of it.

Pure-symbol reveals the higher idea of "relationship" as fundamental in the mystic life. That idea, one might say, is the Rosetta Stone that decodes his mystical universe. "Relational," as I have noted, is a key word in Rielo's genetic metaphysics, and the concept it names is also crucial to the symbolic language of his poetry. Ordinary language is utterly inadequate to describe the state reached by the mystic, the state in which he experiences in intense awareness his *relation* to the whole of universal life. Mystical poetry therefore uses the language of symbols to attempt to capture a "taste" of the ecstasy and the new understanding that attend that experience, as in the following passage from *Llanto azul* in which the poet is speaking to God:

[Nest you are of my tears
and of my laughter.
Nest populated with boldnesses
with immense desires,
with a thousand birds
that, without being born, fly now
through valleys
and mountains...
as if they were seeing you
without seeing you...
That You they embrace
and in You they are deserving

       Soul of always...
       soul of always...!

           may the crossroad

117

sing love, life, death
wing, petal, water
may the tree promise
living leaves, climbing, green...
Yes. Leaves that dreaming, die
to things,
in order to *be* in another way

        but always...
        leaves!]

Nido eres de mis lágrimas
y de mis risas.
Nido poblado de denuedos,
de inmensas ganas,
de mil aves
que, sin nacer, ya vuelan
por valles
y montañas...
Como si te vieran
sin verte...
Que a Ti se abrazan
y en Ti merecen...

        ¡Alma de siempre...
        alma de siempre...!

            que la encrucijada

cante el amor, la vida, la muerte,
el ala, el pétalo, el agua
que el árbol promete
hojas vivas, trepadoras, verdes...
Sí. Hojas que soñando, mueren
a las cosas
para ser de otra manera

        ¡pero siempre ...
        hojas!   (25)

In mystical poetry, as exemplified by the preceding passage, symbols evoke visual imagery based on higher ideas which communicate directly to the emotional center rather than the intellectual center. Esoteric teaching posits that man is asleep or in a state of hypnosis; he is held firmly in the grip of illusion and imagination. It is only the emotional center--the positive emotions of love, hope, and faith--that can awaken him, though unfortunately, in his sleeping state, negative emotions learned by imitation since childhood have blocked access to the true emotional center. Symbolism helps to clear a path to that true emotional center, and thus helps man awaken to his own potential.

Through the mystical symbolism of *raptus* (being taken out of oneself) and *excessus* (going out of oneself), Rielo creates a transformed language of higher consciousness. This language is not that of the ordinary sleeping mind which uses words casually and receives them connotatively, the same word carrying different meanings for each different listener because of the listener's subjective and previously programmed associations to that word. Rather, the symbolic content of Rielo's poetic language is revealed gradually within the context of writing so that there is no question of receiving his words ordinarily, connotatively, and subjectively. Each word or symbol has a figure of meaning to which it refers and with which it confers meaning so that the message is clarified. An example of this withdrawal of language from the subjective-associative thought process might be the following: if the word "rose" is used consistently and repeatedly by a poet throughout an entire poetic work as a figure referring to a happy, joyous sense of perfected beauty, then it can no longer be received with the subjective connotations that might arise from memory, such as the sorrow associated with the roses at your grandmother's funeral, etc... The language of pure-symbol thus becomes something sacred, something that transcends both subjective associations and exoteric organized religion. Rielo's symbolic language of consciousness in his most mystical verses creates a poetry of the active present moment in eternity, where each word has meaning which gradually becomes mutually understood through a unifying energy that binds writer and reader.

Rielo's poetic language is an entire system of redefined, expanded, and interrelated symbols. He does not, of course, prepare a dictionary or notes for the reader; one comes to the meaning of words for this new language by way of reading the entirety of his work and noting through context what these new meanings are. The key to understanding this language lies in the unitive perspective. Normal mind is conditioned to the process of analysis. One ordinarily perceives by positing a split between oneself as the observer, an entity limited by memories and past experiences, and the observed object. The reality, however, is that one *is* one's past; one *is* one's images of things. The unitive seeing that proceeds from awareness of that reality, the mode of vision found in Rielo's work, thus constitutes a process in which the observer and the observed unite. It is a mode of vision without image, without time, without limits--an entrance into a new dimension of time and space. It is seeing with the quality of total awareness, total attention, which is beyond imaging and beyond memory. It is freedom from misery, from boredom, from violence. It is freedom from the isolation of the "self," from the ego's false dreams of itself. There is no conflict in this new dimension; things are revealed as imbued with living energy. The "blue sob" ["*llanto azul*"] of positive emotion--of love, hope, and faith--in another context may figure the weeping, the suffering, the pain and mystical "death" required for change of being to occur. But this positive, unitive sob [*llanto*] of the poet is always a "Yes" ["*Si*"]. This "blue sob" issues from the infinite blue of sky and heaven and the profound blue of the seas: "Yes branches, Yes days, Yes actions, Yes, Yes."

The "blue sob" or "*llanto azul*" is one of the most significant symbols in Rielo's poetry. It is pure-symbol in the sense explained previously, flowing and changing yet ever remaining the same throughout the context of the entire volume of poetry which takes this symbol as its title. In David Murray's bilingual edition of that volume, "*llanto azul*" is translated as "sky blue weeping," which captures the high lyrical intensity of this book. I have chosen "blue sob" as the English rendition, however, for several reasons. First, the difference between "weep" and "sob" (both terms can be used to signify Spanish "*llanto*") is a difference in power: "sob" tends to carry the feeling of a deeper anguish than "weep." Second, the simplicity of "blue," as opposed to "sky blue," allows this adjective to invoke the enormous seas as well as the limitless skies. Moreover, "sky" as a physical phenomenon is quite different from "heaven" as a spiritual state or level of being, and heaven too, no doubt, is one element of this symbol's meaning for Rielo. In the pure-symbol of the "blue sob," the mystic experience is distilled to its purest essence. It is the *Poe'S* of the entire volume of poems to which it gives a name, a force that radiates through each verse. The "blue sob" is the ecstatic thrill of the experience of full consciousness, of "oneness"

120

with all reality: a consciousness of infinity and eternity, a feeling of the whole of the self or real "I" as a part of universal life.

Another mystic pure-symbol that appears frequently in Rielo's work is that of the "kiss," which, like the "touch" of the divine hand in San Juan de la Cruz, figures the moment of entrance into a higher state of consciousness. The kiss marks the consummation of the process of unification with the divine. This symbol is both original and traditional. In many different cultures and eras, the kiss has been read as "the water of life." Rielo maintains this traditional meaning, but adds to it both the idea of mystic union with the divine and the connotations of intimacy, love, and tenderness--qualities inherent in higher states of consciousness but nonetheless derived connotatively from the phenomenological plane of the ordinary experience of love. Rielo thus draws upon the connotations that attend the kiss in ordinary experience in order to make the kiss the pure-symbol of a higher love, a love that springs from the awakened higher emotional center. In the tenderness of a kiss, one's mouth against the mouth of another, one becomes intimate; one touches in tenderness and passion. All barriers, all negatives are removed between those who kiss. In a kiss one unites with another, and a new state is formed in which two are one in love. In Rielo's mystic poems every aspect of the act of kissing is elevated symbolically to define the experience of intimate tender love as one unites through higher consciousness with the divine. The kiss is the act of planting of the mustard seed which becomes like the kingdom of Heaven, filling the whole of oneself with the greatest tree where even birds can make their nests.

Rielo's spiritualizing of the kiss follows the example of those who read *The Song of Songs* as an allegory which presents the Church as the bride of Christ, as the "I" who says, "Let him kiss me with the kisses of his mouth" (1:2). A similar allegory appears in the book of *Revelation*, which refers to "the Bride, the wife of the Lamb" and to "the spirit and the Bride" (21:9, 22:17). And in the writings of the twelfth-century French monk Bernard of Clairvaux, the kiss becomes a figure for the stages of spiritual development, stages enumerated as the purgative, the kiss of the feet; the illuminative, the kiss of the hand; and the unitive, the kiss of the mouth. Bernard also draws heavily on the image of the bride of Christ, most often using it to represent the Church but sometimes to represent the soul of the Christian. He calls his writings, which must be located in the tradition of the "spiritual marriage," a "discourse on love":

Take heed that you bring chaste ears to this discourse on love; and when you think of these two lovers, remember always that not a man and a woman are to be thought of, but the word of God and a soul. And if I shall speak of Christ and the Church, the sense is the same, except that under the name of the Church is specified not one soul only, but the united souls of many, or rather their unanimity. (qtd. in Butler 97)

The following passage from the long poem "Hijo" from *Llanto azul* exemplifies the use of the pure-symbol of the kiss to reflect the mystic experience of the soul uniting with the divine in love. In this passage, God is speaking to the soul of man at the "banquet of Love":

[Son, I am for you
God, Father, Friend
and son if you ask it of me.
I am your beloved
and your lover. You
tell me. If you feel me
Father, all is yours: my kingdom,
my throne
and I myself.

What else
do you desire?

Ask it of me now
and it is yours in this very moment
that you are asleep in your flesh
and awake in my spirit.
Now I give you, not heaven;
yes a *kiss* round like a ball
that entertains a child,
empty and all so it will not be heavy.

Begin.
Push it.
Let it run, let it fly... and in my heart
crash... for I will give it to you
burst into *kisses*
if that consoles you
or amuses you, Yes, son, yours

is the *kiss* of victory
which you deserve,
because you have planted gardens in my heart
that harvest wheat for flowers
and petals for wings.
Like the laborer, son, who, attached to the earth,
mixed with it, stupid and stubborn, strives,
to eat its inner parts.

He has his price
and you... my kisses.]

Hijo, soy para ti
Dios, Padre, Amigo
e Hijo si me lo pides.
Soy tu amado
y tu amante. Tú
me lo dices. Si me sientes
Padre, todo es tuyo: mi reino,
mi trono
y yo mismo.

¿Qué más
quieres?...

Pídelo ahora mismo
y te lo daré en este instante
que estás dormido en tu carne
y despierto en mi espíritu.
Ahora te doy, no el cielo;
sí un beso redondo como pelota
que al niño entretiene.
hueca y todo para que no le pese.

Comienza.
Empújala.
Que corra, que vuele... Y en mi corazón
se estrelle... Que yo te la daré
en besos deshecha,
si eso te consuela

o te divierte. Sí, hijo, tuyo
es el beso del triunfo
que tú mereces
porque has hecho huertos en mi corazón
que cosechan trigo para flores
y pétalos para alas.
Como el labriego, hijo, que apegado a la tierra,
confundido con ella, pueril y terco se afana,
en comer sus entrañas.

        El tiene su precio
        y tú... mis besos.
            (*Llanto azul* 30-31)

In this poem, as in much of Rielo's work, the "kiss" between Father and Son replaces the "marriage" of the husband and the spouse in traditional mysticism. In a presentation delivered at the University of Salamanca in 1979, the *Idente* critics have explored some of the implications of the filial relationship that this poem defines. The *Poe'S* of this poem, they argue, is *Hijo, has sido testigo de mi beso* [Son, you have been witness of my kiss]. The profound intimacy that exists between God the Father and the poet is established as consequence of the divine kiss, which is experienced as ecstacy: *Estás dormido en tu carne / y despierto en mi espíritu* [You are asleep in your flesh / and awake in my spirit]. The colloquial manner in which God manifests himself to the poet is a fundamental feature of Rielo's poetry. The historical precedent for this is found in the most sublime mystic texts like the *Diálogos* of Santa Catalina de Sierra. Such simple, direct language, along with an evocation of the experience of a child, achieves a natural, spontaneous atmosphere in which to bring to light a highly supernatural act of spiritual elevation. This conjunction of apparently diverse aspects contrasts markedly with much previous biblical literature: the divine majesty--without being denied--is transformed into a loving game where God gives himself fully to the human being that he loves. On the other hand, the image of the *labriego* [laborer] establishes a radical distinction between mystical-filial consummation, as personal experience, and the case of men who do not attain that experience. The *Idente* critics believe that this poem expresses with extraordinary clarity the way in which Rielo's role as "witness" of divine love structures both his poetics and his very life (Forés 77).

Another poem that puts to use the pure-symbol of the kiss, along with many of Rielo's other pure-symbols, is "Besos grandes" ["Big Kisses"], which begins:

[Big kisses like cities
are your kisses. Dilated valley
smooth. High mountain range whose summit
is virginal soul, intact.
...

...
O Father. Your sun works the kiss
that on my lip you shine.]

Besos grandes como ciudade
son tus besos. Valle dilatado,
suave. Cordillera que su cima
es alma virginal, intacta.
...

...
Oh Padre. Tu sol trabaja el beso
que en mi labio pules.
(Llanto azul 37)

Since the kiss figures the moment of entrance into the state of divine union, it is closely associated with the higher idea of freedom, with the opening of the doors of the prison of sleep and mechanical life where one can only react and never act. Freedom consists in man's inherited "right" not to be negative, not to hate, not to envy, not to fear. Freedom is the "strongest kiss" of awakening:

[Ah!

Love is the sap that nourishes the air
so that quickly it flies and pushing clouds
to places where the child lives, there, in blue he is.

Oh
child!

Don't halt your step, because, innocent you can't
break your image without breaking your hands
You are, child, like the bird that hurries to see himself *free*.

> That is why,
> you run!

She, like you, from heaven comes.

> From heaven...
> by you seen.

She, like you, teaches the old man
that *freedom* is the strongest kiss
of a lip that conquers a lip.
Your *freedom*, my God summons me
to be in You and your life in me.]

¡Ah!

El amor es savia que al aire nutre
para que de prisa vuele y empujando nubes
a confines que el niño vive, allí, en azul se quede.

> ¡Oh
> niño!

No detienes tu paso, porque, inocente, no puedes
romper tu imagen sin romper tus manos.
Tú eres, niño, como el ave que prisa tiene de verse libre.

> ¡Por eso,
> corres!

Ella, como tú, del cielo viene.

> Del cielo...
> por ti visto.

Ella, como tú, al viejo enseña
que la libertad es el beso más fuerte

de un labio que al labio vence.
Tu libertad, Dios mío, me requiebra
que en Ti me quede y tu vivir me deje.
("Imagen" ["Image"] 74-76)

Here, as elsewhere in Rielo's verse, "child" is symbolic of "innocence"--a godlike quality in man that is strong when one is very young but which one loses as the influences of ordinary life and education put one to sleep. It is this "innocence," this essence, that man must uncover once again. A parallel in esoteric Christianity is the buried conscience, which is an attribute of the awakened emotional center. It is only the recovery and development of this childhood innocence or essence that can bring freedom:

[... the child is new street, new forest
new air, new bird that with its **kiss** signs
and its laugh seals new wings for fulfilled piety.]

... El niño es nueva calle, nuevo bosque,
nuevo aire, nueva ave que con su beso firma
y su risa sella alas nuevas a la piedad cumplida.   (74)

Man can only awaken himself to higher influences, to his own innocence or essence, through effort. This effort is symbolized in Rielo through words like "death," "weep," "sob," and "pain." The suffering denoted by such words makes contact with what is higher in oneself possible. It is through becoming conscious of this suffering that one becomes a conscious man, as the final lines of "Imagen" suggest:

[Oh
Father!

This is something of something that I understood one morning
of rain when your sudden kiss...
that unto death, pale, shouted to me

that one... is not mine!
that one... is not mine!

Oh near weeping that the soul guesses...

that one am I
for you all!]

¡Oh
Padre!

Esto es algo de algo que entendí una mañana
de lluvia cuando tu beso repentino...
que hasta la muerte, pálida, me gritó

¡ése... no es mío!
¡ése... no es mío!

¡Oh lloro cercano que adivina el alma...

eso soy yo
para vosotros!   (76)

In "Imagen" one also finds the pure-symbol of the "bird", through which Rielo figures the upward movement of consciousness or state of being that is part of the process of union with the divine. Birds fly; they enter the vast blue sky. They are not tied to the earth, although they can touch it. They are quick, like the movement into higher consciousness. Like the butterfly, they also represent the completely distinctive nature of higher consciousness. Higher levels of being are not just bigger and better caterpillar attributes; higher being is the butterfly. Metamorphosis occurs; what was, is no longer. A new creature has emerged; quality has been transformed, not quantity. The bird in Rielo symbolizes this process of metamorphic change in being. The bird flies: its reality, its world, its perspective, its environment, its total being are of a a new and different quality.

"Wings" are another pure-symbol in Rielo's language of mysticism. Wings have all the symbolic qualities of the bird but constitute its quintessence. They symbolize the potential inherent in man to lift himself higher on the scale of being. They are closely linked to the available inward seed of the biblical parable, the seed that man can grasp and plant and water, and thus further symbolize the very essence of spirit in man. They are also closely linked to the scriptural simile which states that the word of God is as "sharp as a two-edged sword, that renders even the spirit from the soul." The word of God, God himself, entering man, wounds him with love, the sharp sword severing the soul from the spirit. This severing is figured in Rielo's poetry by wings. Wings thus become a symbol for the soul freed and united simultaneously with the divine, God, the Source of All, the Absolute--the soul being the element in man that he shares with God, "*la llama viva de amor*" ["the living flame of love"], as it was figured by the classic Spanish mystic San Juan de la Cruz. In Rielo, the pure-symbol of the bird figures the metapmorphosis of the spirit as it strives for higher consciousness, while the pure-symbol of wings represents both the potential for upward flight and the fulfilment of that potential--the essence, the spirit, Love itself, God in man: *Las alas que gemido llevan / son almas* [The wings that carry moans / are souls] ("Alas" ["Wings"] 8).

The pure-symbol of the "flower" in Rielo's poetry figures the qualities of tenderness and beauty generated by the higher intellectual and higher emotional centers functioning in the mystic state. The mystic man sees himself as a part of all that is and sees all that is as part of himself, a vision that moves him to tenderness, to profound compassion. The emotions and compulsions of lower states of man-- violence, conflict, envy, jealousy, self-seeking, self-importance--fall away. Man's reason passes from subjective to objective; his centers of feeling, thinking, and moving are balanced. The essence of reality becomes visible; the beauty of life itself is unveiled.

Color is one of the most significant pure-symbols in Rielo's poetry, and the importance Rielo attributes to color is unprecedented in the tradition of Spanish mystical poetry. Color fuses with the sense of hearing to become "sound" and finally expands in meaning to include the "feeling" of deeply sensed love. In "Lirios de junio" ["June Lilies"], these "sounds" and "feelings" of "color" speak through the *innocence* (pure-symbol of man's essence as opposed to personality) of lilies with God's voice; the theme of this speaking is mystic death and rebirth:

[Lilies
innocent
Lilies
lovers
Lilies those... those You, oh Father brought to me
to speak through them the life
that you dreamed, the death you chose.

You did it with *sounds* of clear color:
whites, blues, rose, yellows...
tender colors in my trembling love.]

Lirios
inocentes.
Lirios
amantes.
Lirios aquellos... aquellos que Tú, oh Padre, me venías
para hablar por ellos el vivir
que soñabas, la muerte que escogías.
Lo hacías con sonidos de colores claros:
blancos, azules, rosa, amarillos...
colores tiernos en mi amor tembloroso.　　(90)

In the last lines of this same poem, the pure-symbol color is
redefined as the truth of immortal life:

[The lilies upright, flowing with sap, ecstatic
I ... attentive to color
that does not die, is not annihilated.
No. No. Color is not death nor ire.
Color is truth of someone who comes.
Truth of life that never ends.]

Los lirios erguidos, jugosos, extáticos.
Yo ... atento al color
que no muere, que no aniquila.
No. No. El color no es muerte ni es ira.
El color es la verdad de alguien que viene.
La verdad de la vida que nunca fenece.　　(90)

In addition to the technique of pure-symbolism, the lyrical
metamorphosizing of words also plays a fundamental role in Rielo's
language of consciousness. Words become something other than what
they have been. They are transformed for new acts, new life; their very
quality is changed. Language becomes a function of transformational
aesthetics. One of the primary means through which such
metamorphosis takes place is through the consistent presonification
of certain words. The color blue, for example, sobs or weeps. The

emotional intensity of profound sadness that reaches the peak of crying aloud is attributed to the color blue. This process is also, however, more than mere personification. Blue is the predominant color visible to our perception of the world. Both the sky above us and the sea which covers the vast majority of the planet earth are blue. Thus, the color blue is itself an enormous presence in our world, although in ordinary states, we are only vaguely aware of it. In Rielo's work, this enormous presence, blue, though not corporeal, sobs; it cries out in anguish. The scope of this enormous presence of blue raises the process of personification to metamorphosis. Blue is not simply a color; it is the world, the height of the heavens and the depth of the seas, both of which are inaccessible to man, both beyond the reach of man. Blue's sob is thus the deep, familiar expression of pain--the pain of the known and the unknown, the pain of knowing and not knowing, the pain of fear, the pain of death, the pain of sleep of mechanical man as he stands in the world with the seed of light and consciousness within, unplanted, and unwanted. Blue is not personified by sobbing, nor is the sob described by its blueness. A metamorphosis of language has taken place. Language has lyrically encompassed metaphysics, standing as pure-symbol of the reality of being. An example is found in the poem "Nadie viene" ["No one comes"]:

[Oh blue, that refreshes misfortunes
and with your shine, distancing punishment, leave us water!
You are, oh water! the Light of the Pilgrim.
When at its zenith the road is reached
and, converted into a fragile dot,
to dream you leave us...

        that die we may...
        to ourselves.]

¡Oh azul, que refrescas infortunios
y con tu brillo, alejando castigos, agua nos dejas!
Tú eres, ¡oh agua!, la luz del peregrino,
cuando cenital el camino alcanza
y, convertido en frágil punto,
soñar nos deja...

que morir podemos...
a nosotros mismos.   (15)

The reality of the wish to be is that one must die to what one was before.   There is pain, struggle and effort in this transformation. Rielo's mysticism establishes this esoteric truth through the pure-symbol constituted by the two words *llanto azul*.

Another important technique of lyrical metapmorphosis for Rielo is the coining of neologisms. In "Lirios de junio" ["June Lilies"], for example, Rielo uses the word "*eyo*" to refer to the real "I," the deepest, most intimate part of the self, the essence or seed of "congenuity." It is the *eyo* that lives after the death of the ego, which was formed by life. Behind the *eyo* stands God, so Rielo figures the eyo in "Lirios de junio" as *mi cáliz de amores lleno* [my chalice full of loves] (90). The sacred quality of the *eyo* is revealed in the word "chalice," which in traditional Christianity is the holy cup that holds the blood of Christ through which humanity will be saved. The *eyo* is "attentive"; it possesses the quality of attention or awareness that esoteric teachings hold sacred, since it is this quality alone that can awaken man from his hypnotized sleep: "I... attentive to color". The *eyo* is acquired by suffering:

[Oh birth of sob, of fertil sob
in lilac soul that moistens the high powerful breezes.
Oh prompt heaven... I offered you my *eyo*
that awaited my personal arrival... my chalice
filled with loves, pouring into You.
You were telling me...
with your finger against my lip: -Son, rest.
You *are* a lily that lives me dead.]

Oh parto del llanto, del llanto fértil
en alma lila que moja las altas brisas poderosas.
Oh cielo presuroso... Yo te ofrecía lo que era eyo
en espera que mi personal llegada... mi cáliz
de amores lleno, en Ti derramara.
Tú me decías...
con tu dedo en mi labio: -Hijo, descansa.
Ya lirio eres que me vive muerto.

The inattentive I's of ego are legion. Each small "I" has its desire, its dream, its emotion, its thought. Many contradict each other. Each has only self-interest as reality. It is in great part this lack of unity that keeps man mechanical. In a poem from *Balcón a la bahía*, Rielo speaks of the nature of the ego:

> [Who has not violated the innocence of a tear?
> The ego does not respect:
>
> > nor blood gathered in glass
> > nor some feet sheltered between seeking hands
>
> The ego imposes dense borders without greatness
> and is unaware of the shadow hidden in love that ennobles.
>
> Of myself I only know that, on the secret day
> when I give birth to announced death
> sure in truth that I have died,
> with my blind sorrows...
>
> > I will not shout my name!]

> ¿Quién no ha violado la inocencia de una lágrima?
> El egoísmo no respeta:
>
> > ni la sangre reunida en vaso
> > ni unos pies cobijados entre manos solícitas.
>
> El egoísmo impone densas fronteras sin grandeza
> e ignora la escondida enamorada sombra que ennoblece.
>
> De mí yo sólo sé que, en el secreto día,
> cuando dé a luz la muerte anunciada,
> firme en verdad que he muerto,
> con mis segadas penas...
>
> > ¡no gritaré mi nombre!
> > > (*Balcón a la bahía* 75)

Aside from the deep understanding it demonstrates of the obstacles posed by the ego for a man who wishes to *be*, this poem illustrates one of the characteristics that ensure the enduring value of Rielo's poetry: real sensibility and tenderness combined with

133

compassion and love. In the first line this quality is resplendent: "who has not violated the innocence of a tear?"

The quality in man that Rielo hopes to recover--his innocence, the child in him, *eyo*--is a dominant motif in his poems. The "tear" is a symbol of that real emotion of which man is capable but which somehow gets buried by the process of ordinary education and the influences of quotidian life until all that is available is the ego, a complex of vanity, pride, self-love, envy, and hatred. The child in man buries his innocence or essence because of a very unfortunate element in his nature: suggestibility and imitation.

Yet another technique of lyric metamorphosis consists in the compounding of the significance of the thing signified in the symbol, a densifying of imagery through which many ideas are expressed in few words. Thus, what in less profound poetry would be merely personification becomes pure symbol in mystic poetry. Rielo's poetry abounds with this metamorphosizing quality. Everything, every feeling, every act or result of action is infused with *La Llama Viva* or "The Living Flame." His mystical language of consciousness brings to life everything that it names: time, rocks, sky, earth. In that language even a tiny individual tear becomes the universal tear, and any tree may become the Tree of Life in the midst of the garden to the east of Eden. Thought is *felt* as deep emotion. The sacred force of attention is focused simultaneously on both mind and feeling.

Rielo explains the creation of a new language of consciousness that includes the sense of sight to express the inexpressible when he writes: *la mirada tersa / es palabra clara que despliega alas* [the flowing glance / is clear word that spreads wings]. The full meaning of this clause becomes clearer in context:

[Let me take your hand; and whole on my chest,
like an emerald, hanging from the oh
that does not sleep if you don't wound it
may it harass your night, fallen ground, so that it will never live
again
the beggar fear that purple afflicts.
Forget your feet as well. The flowing glance
is clear word that spreads wings.
Leave the earth as well. The earth suffices
for dead clay jars.]

Deja que tome tu mano; y entera en mi pecho,
como una esmeralda, colgante del ay
que no duerme si no lo hieres
afane tu noche, caído suelo, para que nunca reviva
el mendigo miedo que lo cárdeno aflige.
Olvida también los pies. La mirada tersa
es palabra clara que despliega alas.
Deja también la tierra. La tierra basta
para tinajas muertas.

(*Llanto azul* 81)

Entera [whole] becomes a verb with the qualities of an emerald.
The sign of wonder "oh" becomes an object, a form from which the
emerald hangs; one notes the personification of this word of
exclamation, more like a sigh, becoming object. It can be wounded and
it can act. In this same stanza, the emotional state of fear is also
personalized: it is a beggar afflicted by purple. Thus color also acts.
The symbol of the beggar expresses the esoteric teaching of the
necessity of purification of the emotional center by complete removal
of all negative emotions, the greatest of which is fear, in order to clear
a space for higher emotion. Even God the Father Himself undergoes
metamorphosis in Rielo's verse. God becomes "tears" wept by the hand
of the poet:

[I weep you, O father that my hand that holds the goldfinch
may water life and ignore death.]

Te lloro oh Padre que mi mano que el jilguero sostiene
riegue la vida e ignore la muerte.   (83)

A few other important stylistic elements of Rielo's language
include the following:

The use of nouns as adjectives: "down pupil"; "sun laughter" (87);
"water night"; "invalid star" (83); "water voice" (42); "moon honey"
(96).
The personification of ideas, concepts and actions: "Secrets Stroll,
weighless, hand in fortunate hand"; "smiling dreams" (82); "The
kiss listens" (39); "...dreams that sail on a tear / to be ideas that into
kisses merge to be blued" (29); "death dies" (24); "death is lived by
the sea" (29)

135

Personification of inanimate objects: "Tired nests" (82); "Noble corners" (44); "Sad table" (94)

Personification of parts of the body: "New lips that never stop coming" (82); "... this hand of mine that lies twice dead, breaking the quick worlds of other hands" (83); "The heart moans with cold and love" (34) "Blood weeps color" (95).

Personal physical characteristics and occurrences, such as a blush, take on the attributes of water or liquid: "Tepid blush" (82); "milky foot" (93).

The plural noun often takes a singular verb: "The kisses that beings describes" (83); "oceans creates"; "heavens flies" (60); "Blues convokes" (93).

Present participles function as adjectives: "Raining night" (83); "Thinking water" (61); "Falling golds" (64).

The surprising combinations of words that produce or form new ideas: "Total afternoon" (85); "lived transparency" (29); "Dry water" (98); "Soul with her tear open" (29); "weeping weeps" (61).

The ascribing of human features, or organs, or feelings, to things in the world of nature: "Quiet garden full of lips" (85); "kiss in breezes" (94); "Shadows taste of pine" (68); "light bleeds" (96); "petals caress" (96); "Saddened sun" (98).

The animation of color: "fallen blues" (83); "tender color" (90); "its voice disposed toward rose-color" (29).

Everything lives in Rielo's verse. Everything is infused with life: the animate, the inanimate, feelings, thoughts. All vibrate with life. The following verse is one example:

[The sky is cold steel.
Its sheeting is afternoon
that my retreat its heartbeat hides.
Retreat of natural solitudes
in dark furrows that weeping tills,
that weeping tills...

when the soul is oh buried or unarmed
in the breast, that, aching stone, still, ductile, seals,
Like water that begets souls
for happy tender shining stars.]

El cielo está acero frío.
Su lámina es tarde
que el retiro mío su latido esconde.
Retiro de soledades naturales
en pardos surcos que labra el lloro,
que labra el lloro...
cuando el alma es ay enterrado o inerme
en el pecho, que, lápida doliente, quieto, dúctil sella.
Como agua que engendra almas
para felices luceros tiernos.   (85)

The sense of all-pervasive, all-infusing life is created by what I will
call Rielo's "imageless imagery"--the imagery engendered by the
contemplative state in which the arrow of attention is double. In this
state, the poet is aware of "himself" and at the same time becomes part
of the phenomena observed. The barrier of the *images* of the self in
the ordinary state of consciousness is removed, allowing the poem's
images to evoke a unitive life-force that underlies and ultimately calls
into question distinctions of subject and object. The poem's
reverberations, its *Poe'S*, issue from the elevated state of being of the
poet. The poet's thought is quiet, so quiet that it expands into immense
space, thus dissolving the small "silk" which in ordinary states of
consciousness remembers past pleasure and pain. The prison doors
are opened; the sacred comes into view. The poem thus issues from
this state of attentive awareness--of simultaneity, presence and
participation. Through the creation of the poem, the mind empties
itself of itself. Mystic union occurs.

The necessity of self-study in order to know objective reality and
reach a higher level of the self is the   understanding that Rielo's
language of consciousness imparts. One hears the whisper of the
ancient inscription on the temple of Delphi: "Know thyself and thou
will know the universe and the Gods." The poet is an impartial witness
of himself in his intimate relation to the world of spirit and the world
of nature. He collects whole albums which show him what he is; like a
photographer he catches characteristics, emotions, postures, thoughts.

If the reader enters this observing, aware presencing, he will *see* that his usual perception of self has little to do with reality. He will understand that it is not enough to see himself as others see him, and as he imagines himself. He will understand that there is much that is artificial in him, that he must divide what is real in himself from what is not. He must see himself as he *is*. In his book of proverbs *Transfiguraciones* [Transfigurations]) Rielo writes: "If you wish to become wise, dwell upon the mystery you are" (84).

"Light" is the pure-symbol of consciousness and awakening in Rielo's poetry: one sees where before one was blind. This symbol usually is found in close proximity to the "kiss," the mystical touch or consummation between the soul and God:

[There...
In paradise of nascent angels
like a multitude of sudden birds,
unexpected, soft, lucid lovers of a kiss
that to the kiss... their kiss they gave
and in kiss remained... remained awake.
Awake dreaming on the marine plane
bathed in lights...
that the happy dawn repeats.

       Yes, Father.]

Allí...
En paraíso de ángeles nacientes
como multitud de aves repentinas,
súbitas, suaves, amantes lúcidas de un beso
que al beso... su beso dieran
y en beso quedara... quedara despierto,
despierto soñando en el altiplano marino
bañado en luces...
que la aurora dichosa repite.

       Sí, Padre.
            (*Llanto azul* 105-106)

Later in the same poem light becomes a flame, a symbol revealing the transfigurative qualities of the state of higher awareness. This "flame," however, is also the wing of a swan, one of the largest, most beautiful birds on earth, a bird which since ancient times has been associated with impartial love:

[Oh smile of yours of unbroken profile
and open to the thirsty hand of a lip
that without repose asks for that it desires:

The flame of a wing
in the feather of a swan.]

Oh sonrisa la tuya de perfil nunca quebrado
y abierta a la mano sedienta de un labio
que sin reposo pide aquello que ansía:

La llama de un ala
en la pluma de un cisne.   (106)

This flame is a sign not only of light and warmth but also of man's true heart, the heart that radiates and emanates energy derived from a higher level than itself. The flame's manifestation in "the feather of a swan" is an expanded symbol of the lightness of freedom and the beauty that man attains when he stands revealed as the image of God and God's essence: love. The key to this transformation is the desire to *be* "without repose." This desire, which is expressed again and again in Rielo's poems, in context acquires the power of "the flame" or "spark."

In the same poem, glimpses of a world that is beyond sleep are signified by such light-related terms and images as "brilliance," "stars," and "mirror," as well as by verbs that refer to sight and clarity:

[Days, oh, of oval mirror
where I would see the living portrait
of your sweet smile
... ...
... reaching in flight
the pure blue, rapt and weightless, of a kiss
that sweetly clarifies it and leaves it in brilliance.]

139

Días, ay, de ovalado espejo
que yo veía el vivo retrato
de tu dulce sonrisa.
... ...
... en vuelo alcance
el puro azul, raptado y sin peso, de un beso,
que dulce lo aclare y en brillo quede.   (105)

In a poem called "Trino" ("Trill"), the same images are present but
here the other world beyond sleep becomes the "eye that cries for the
lover it longs for." The symbols here are almost impressionistic in the
painterly sense:

[I know of a bird traced in pencil that glitters the cry
of a kiss that lives alone. Yes, alone. Alone
in the rapt dream of a nest of intimate shining stars
that the hasty mist dresses in the secret of itself.
In it I remain the brief instant of a sigh
that exhales world filled with universes; a world
like the eye that cries to the lover it longs for.
That world is not this one... this one
that I live
and with my feet
traverse.
And there, You. You and your gesture.
Yes, that is it; your gesture, looking at me
for me to look at you, and then...]

Yo sé de un ave trazada a lápiz que rutila el lloro
de un beso que vive solo. Sí. Solo. Solo
en el raptado sueño de un nido de luceros íntimos
que la bruma presurosa viste en el secreto de sí misma.
En él me quedo el breve instante de un suspiro
que exhala de mundo de universos lleno; un mundo
como el ojo que grita al amante que ansía.
ese mundo no es éste... éste
que vivo
y con mis pies
recorro.
Y allí, Tú. Tú y tu gesto.

Sí, eso es; tu gesto, mirándome
que yo te miro, y luego...   (102)

The symbol of light is expressed with the feeling of intense love.
Power and energy radiate from this symbol: God is the presence of
light:

[They will fly the intense clarities of new lights
that colors of untouchable mirrors modulate...
if they touch. Ah, if they touch...]

Volarán los claros intensos de luces nuevas
que colores de espejos intocables modulan...
Si se tocan. Ah, si se tocan...   (101)

The symbol of light branches semantically in several directions,
drawing into its sphere all other words that cannot exist apart from the
idea of light: brilliance, stars, sparkle, etc. The idea of "seeing more"
or being conscious of more may thus be expressed by any one of these
many words or images. In the symbol of light, as with Rielo's other
symbols, the lines between nouns, verbs, and adjectives are blurred.
The magic power of words is restored.

Pure essence as pure-symbol, from Rielo's ontological
perspective, is the "cross" as in the "Cross of Christ." The inner esoteric
message is, "I am the resurrection and the life," the words through
which Christ refers to the death of personality and the emergence of
life in essence. The essence of the Radiant Presence is expressed in
the pure-symbol "blue" and its plural "blues." (However, in Spain
"blues" does not have the negative aspect of sadness which American
English has inherited from Black culture, especially in the form of
music. Modern jazz, for example, was born of the "blues," as in the
music of B.B. King, John Coltrane, and Miles Davis.) In Spanish
mysticism "blue" figures the enfolding light that lifts one into presence,
the *Anima* of the *Animus*, the transverberation of divine joy and
impartial human love. In ancient civilizations this impartial love
passed, as symbol, into the infrastructure of the aesthetic field where
it is invisibly protected against any imperfect suggestions (Saint
Germain). The final expansion of the pure-symbol blue is found in one
of Rielo's unpublished sonnets from a collection called *Sombras
Vírgenes [Virgin Shadows]*:

141

[I with my hands and their gesture direct
the traffic of my dawn that repairs
solitudes of my blue child's jump
upon the leaves of my severely punished soul.

Lonlinesses encircle my wounded kisses
seeing them wakes of piercing tears
that, moulded into gauze of wheat martyr
offering bread without field, become altar

I have seen you, Christ, hidden with my crosses
of living fire burning with your messiah like
sufferings abundant suffering, sealed

destiny to which, purified, you carry me...
as a crown of a promised kingdom.
How I have dreamed, my Christ, to be with you!]

Yo con mis manos y su gesto dirijo
el tráfico de mi aurora que repara
soledades de mi azul salto de niño
sobre la fronda de mi alma fustigada.

Soleados circulan mis besos heridos
viéndolos estelas de pungentes lágrimas
que, amasándose en cendales de mártir trigo
ofrecido pan sin campo, hácense ara.

Te he visto, Cristo, escondido con mis cruces
de vivo fuego ardiendo con tus mesiánicos
dolores, dolor ubérrimo, sellado

destino al que, purificado, me llevas...
para corona de un reino prometido.
¡Cuánto he soñado, mi Cristo, ser contigo!   (n. pag.)

"Blue" is the signifier, while "innocence" or "essence" as "child" is
the signified. Transubstantiation occurs with the "bread" without
fields, "the body of Christ" *signifier* + *signified* as the destiny of man:
the crown of the promised "kingdom of Heaven" within man as higher
emotional and intellectual centers, real conscience and real "*I*" behind

which stands God. *Blue* is thus pure-symbol of freedom from *alteración* in its true etimological meaning explained from the Spanish perspective very clearly by the philosopher and essayist Ortega y Gasset, who is an important influence on all twentieth Century writers from Spain. Ortega stated in a paper delivered in Buenos Aires in 1939:

> Our Spanish word *otro* [other] is nothing but the Latin *alter*. To say, then, that the animal lives not from *itself* but from what is *other* than itself, pulled and pushed and tyrannized over by that *other*, is equivalent to saying that the animal always lives in estrangement, is beside itself, that its life is essential *alteración* [alteration]. (Ortega y Gasset, 393)

Ortega later refers to this *alteración* as "the infrahuman torpor which primitive man continues in part," and he reiterates the idea of man as a self-developing creation in discussing "gifts of higher powers": Nothing that is substantive has been conferred upon man. He has to do it all himself (395). Ortega maintains that the nomenclature for man inherited from Linaeus and the eighteenth century--*homo sapiens*--is not an expression of good faith, since it falsely intimates that man knows all he needs to know. He suggests that the proper nomenclature should be *homo insipiens*. He applauds Plato, who defines man by his ignorance. Rielo's mystical depiction of "man asleep" in the illusion of powers he only thinks he possesses is in harmony with this important aspect of Ortega y Gasset's philosophy.

Rielo elevates this philosophy to symbolic language through empirical mystical poetry, poetry energized (like all great mystical poetry) by a special upward channeling of the powerful sex force. The vow of celibacy transmutes the sex force into a spiritual force released in the form of mental creativity and epigenisis, a force manifested in impartial love and conscious Being.

Rielo affirms the living force of God in man and man in God through his "Yes." His poems are abundant with the positive emotions of higher being: love, hope, and faith which he raises to the level of symbol with the word "yes." Everything in his poetic vision falls under the magic of this positive energizing emotion: branches, birds, actions. The following are a few examples of this fundamental, expansive symbol of positive emotion. The dialogue as always is with God.

143

[*Yes*, mine...
That does not cry, nor laugh, nor sing... *Yes* flies
to the sweet region that doves make
for their flights, not here... *Yes* in the soul
of he who does not kill them to be happy.]

sí, mía...
que no llora, no ríe, no canta... *Sí* vuela
a la dulce región que palomas hace
para ser voladas, no aquí... *Sí* en el alma
de quien no las mata para ser feliz.
(Llanto azul 78)

[*Yes* in my beloved valley, where your profile
by me seen, tells me, me, tireless traveler
of blues: yours is my path. Follow it to the end.

And the end I see it.
It is You!

You are what I love!]

Sí en mi valle amado, donde tu perfil
por mí visto, me dice, a mí, viajero incansable
de azules: tuyo es mi sendero. Síguelo hasta el fin.

Y el fin lo veo.
¡Eres Tú!

¡Tú eres lo que amo yo!   (69)

In *Llanto azul*, as the passages quoted in the preceding pages show,
Rielo's syntax displays a certain disregard for the structures and
categories dictated by standard grammar. There is a "verbness" in his
nouns, putting them into action and taking them through time; there is
a "nounness" in his verbs, giving them new dimensions. The limited
signs of language are stretched and transformed in an effort to
designate infinite reality. The result is a kaleidoscopic pattern where
the meanings of words and symbols are suggested not only by inherent
qualities but even more by their relations with other words used
throughout the whole of the poet's work. The normal usage of

language is broken in order to enable the reader to understand things differently and, more importantly, to begin to feel things in a positive way.[1] The concepts of matter and form, time and space are altered by Rielo's use of language. These concepts, no matter how "natural" they may seem, do not constitute the fundamental law that governs the operations of language. For Rielo's language is dictated instead by the sacred laws of God, whose presence is the light of consciousness and whose essence is impartial love.

In relation to its theme, Rielo's style can best be categorized as mystical symbolism. His thematic message is that of esoteric Christianity, and his language calls into play a mystical, plasteresque surrealism. That language creates a purposeful shock by displacing objects, phenomena, noumena, actions, and all the semantic references possible in poetry into extraordinary, totally incongruous syntactic positions. This brings about a new way of thinking, a way of deconstructing the patterned, mechanical thinking that Gurdjieff's metaphysics terms "fomatory thinking" (Ouspensky, *Fourth Way* 345). Thus one observes that form and content in Rielo's poetics are in perfect harmony, both giving rise to attention, consciousness and unity.

There may be many words, many uses of those words, and indeed many different languages, but there is only *one* meaning. For Rielo, meaning is not engendered by language but rather precedes language. Symbolic Language aims at this meaning, and its aim becomes the unifying element that makes understanding possible. If that aim is true, language becomes a language of the heart, a language of pure meaning. The characteristic features of Rielo's use of language throughout all his work are intensity, passion, and presence. His principal tool is symbolism and his aim is consciousness of the infinite, all-pervading presence of God.

---

1. The style of Rielo's later poetry, as in the volumes Balcón a la bahía and Dolor entre cristales, varies. It is less impressionistic and the use of symbolism is not as pronounced. However, the tone, objectives, and themes of the poems in these volumes are the same as in Llanto azul.

VI

Major Theme

Destiny
As Death And Suffering

"Whispers of heavenly death--Darest thou--Now--O soul--walk
out with me toward the unknown Region--where neither ground
is for the feet nor any path to follow?"
                                    Walt Whitman (399)

"The Lord is nigh unto them that are of a broken heart and serveth
such as be of a contrite Spirit." (Ps. 51:17)

The one and only theme in Rielo's poetry is Destiny. "Destiny"
here means an active participation in life, as opposed to the forces of
fate or accident over which the individual apparently has no control
and which constitute the law of undeveloped man. Man's destiny is to
unite with the celestial Father in presence and being and thus view
earth from Heaven rather than Heaven from earth. As Marie Lise
Gazarian-Gautier writes of Rielo's work: "His poetry is a visible
account of that invisible round trip journey--earth, heaven,
earth--which the soul has undertaken" (n. pag.).

The immortal search for the transcendental goes on almost
unnoticed in today's world of technocracy. Continual technological
"progress" promotes the illusion that man has already attained a
completely developed consciousness, and authentic ideas of man's true
ontological and spiritual nature have faded and are disappearing.
Language no longer reflects the ancient understandings. Thus the poet
and mystic, whose mission is to revive the language and verity of such

146

authentic ideas, is a modern hero in the true sense of the word. It is time, indeed it is urgent, for these truths to be known, before it is too late and the human species as we know it, is no more. Rielian genetic metaphysics reveals the great law of Being that begins and ends in God. The absolute creator moves downward into all life, engendering the potential for self-development and evolution. "Sleeping man" does not perceive this law; he sees only the material, external forms of creation. The influences and impressions of ordinary life cannot change his view, his limited, "sleeping" understanding. Only conscious "shocks," such as impressions evoked by the art works and literary works of conscious beings, can begin to awaken him. All the great mystics have taught that shocks must begin with a *new perception of the self*. The "external man" must be made passive so that the "essence," that substance received in man at birth from above, from the starry world of God, can begin to "hear" the messages from higher centers within one's being, centers which are already in place, already developed, but unconnected. When these higher centers become active, when they are not shut off by the constant turnings of the lower centers, by negative emotion and associative mechanical thought, they receive messages and energy directly from higher consciousness. The illusions of life end. One attains a new understanding of one's true nature and one's part in the law of Being emanating from God the Father. One's sole aim becomes truth, the power of conscious being. This state of being is poetically a "place" within the self, a place where the "new self" born from the death of personality becomes the real heart and axis within. From this place higher emotions "go forth" from man and make contact with forces beyond the level of sleep. This contact or mystical union is not reserved for the few, but is available to all men. Passion emerges from this contact or "union" as a strong desire for Being (as the definition of mystic death in the lower centers). This passion becomes the catalyst of intentionality and awareness whereby one's essence can be sensed. There is no contact, no union, without suffering, without *el llanto* for the animal one is in ordinary conciousness. This *llanto* is the purifying fire of sacrifice and is necessary for the birth of higher feelings: love, hope, and faith.

The title of Rielo's most recent volume of verse *Dolor entre cristales* [Pain within panes] is a symbol of the process of suffering that man undergoes in the search to fulfill his destiny. The *cristales* [panes or windows] are made of *dolor* [suffering] which reflects the unknown to man's inner vision. They thus reveal the forces of the sacred laws of creation in the universal dimension, the forces which man must activate within himself. The vast difference between what man is and what he can become must be paid for with pain. There is no possibility of something for nothing in this search for truth. Moreover, payment must be made in advance. The seeker must pass through "the dark night of the soul" which is the total realization of the exact nature of his sleep and the absolute acceptance of the fact that his ordinary life has been little better than that of an animal or a machine. The ascetic imperative is law; the purifying fire of conscious suffering is the pain of struggle with the lower self.

The meanings evoked by a symbol, for Rielo as for any other poet, are multiple and call forth different levels of reference. *Cristales*, for example, means not only "windows" but also "crystals" in Spanish. Taking into account Rielo's vast knowledge of myth, the idea of ancient teachings regarding the healing power of crystals in the hands of a priest cannot be dismissed. The capacity of crystal to refract light--breaking the whole white light into the seven colors of the spectrum, a process illustrated most spectacularly in nature by the rainbow--makes it a powerful symbol. In the Scriptures, the rainbow, the arch from heaven to earth, is a symbol of the covenant between God and man. At the ordinary level of reference, "window" is the object before which one stands in order to see in or to see out: the passage of seeing. And on still another level the image of pain within/between crystals/windows suggests seeing through a glass darkly--the double, or *redoublement*, as barrier. Yet the "substance" of the crystal windows is the two-ended stick of suffering: mechanical suffering which must be undone, and intentional suffering, the suffering that occurs when one meets with awakened sight the animal in himself, struggles against it with the pain of remorse, and finally puts it to death. In a poem from this volume we read:

[The houses wanted to have been trees
that death went piercing little by little.

Impossible desire because pain only
can, truthful, reveal a man.

Pain unites with no one
all blood in flight has its own moment.

The rest, afterwards: indivisible hand
is a new heaven because it is always new.]

Las casas querrían haber sido árboles
que la muerte va talando poco a poco.

Deseo imposible porque el dolor sólo
puede, verdadero, decirse del hombre.

El dolor con nadie se une:
toda sangre en vuelo tiene propio instante.

Lo demás, después: mano indivisible
es un cielo nuevo porque siempre es nuevo.

(Dolor entre cristales 42)

The most exquisite of Fernando Rielo's poetry is found in his unpublished book of sonnets titled *Sombras vírgenes* [Virgin Shadows]. The purity and perfection of his verse in this difficult structure is reflected in the extraordinary title. In this manuscript, the theme of death and immortality as seen from the perspective of conscious Being exerts a tremendous power, functioning as a shock to the intuitive center for those who "have ears to hear":

[It has no being death with its dead
nothing more we know now of death;
and of the dead, only that they have lived.
The earth makes them hers, she works them.

Until its pure naked nakedness
escapes from the sepulchre to place
some flowers in a cloud of memory
what only wither in a short time.

Another dying exists: that of oneself
through a God of life that becomes ecstasy
if we judge our soul loathsome:

just judgement of the just with whom the Judge unites
because in this way is justice newly wed:
two beings transposing their being.]

No tiene ser la muerte con sus muertos.
Ya nada más sabemos de la muerte;
y de los muertos, sólo que han vivido.
La tierra hácelos suyos, los trabaja.

Hasta su pura desnudez desnuda
escapa del sepulcro para en nube
del recuerdo poner algunas flores
que en tiempo breve a solas se marchitan.

Existe otro morir: el de uno mismo
por un Dios de la vida que se hace éxtasis
si juzgamos nuestra alma aborrecible:

justo juicio del justo al que el Juez se une
porque así es la justicia desposada:
dos seres traspasándose su ser.   (n. pag.)

In death, the soul escapes; The soul is naked nakedness: the
essence of essence stripped clean and pure of all that covered it.
This death is the mystic "death in life," the *otro morir* [other dying]
that becomes ecstasy when one attains understanding of one's
origin in the starry world. This understanding is the most powerful
thing that man can gain.

The mystical imagery is powerful and precise, imbued with
conscious energy of a rare quality which reveals within the language
itself the sacred law from higher mind: "just judgement of the just with
whom the Judge unites." One must work for Being; one must struggle
and conquer one's lower animal nature to become a real man. The
legions of passing, contradictory thoughts and feelings must be seen
for what they are; then they must die. Unified "I," the "I" of essence,
must control, must live. Behind this "I," embracing this real "I," is God:
"two beings transposing their being." The mystical metamorphosis in
being is complete. Objective reality comes into view. The long-buried
consciences is vivified and becomes active. Higher emotional and
intellectual centers work together in harmony. Objective reason, and
positive emotions of love, hope, and faith are actualized in man. Man's
origin, his genetic metaphysical reality, is comprehended; and his
destiny, the self-developing potential for psychological evolution, for
higher states of consciousness, is fulfilled. Man has walked through
the gates of the temple of Delphi. He has walked the inner paths of his

own invisible world and "become known" to himself. In this knowledge he has also known "the universe" and "the gods." This is the message of empirical mysticism. It is not theory; rather, it is the practice here and now of work for Being.

Rielo introduces his volume of sonnets with the following words:

[Man is created by God in order to learn
     to say farewell to the world: his last look
         is, for this reason, the only thing that does not end in
                ashes.]

El hombre es por Dios creado para que por sí aprenda
     del mundo a despedirse: su postrera mirada
     es, por eso, lo único que no acaba en ceniza.
           (*Sombras vírgenes* n.pag.)

The message is clear: man's destiny is to be a creation of God, an experiment in self-development. The paradox of mystical "life in death," the death of the body as the beginning of the circle, "life-death", on the level of eternity--all are concepts impossible to know in ordinary mind. One must begin to awaken through ideas imparted by conscious beings. Then empirical personal experience may bring real understanding.

"His last look / is, for this reason, the only thing that does not end in ashes": man's "last look" constitutes a metaphorical *redoublement* of death--the death of personality on the level of ordinary life, and the death of the body on the higher level of eternity. These deaths leave, as the only thing that is not destroyed, "that does not end in ashes," the essence or higher consciousness: real "I" on the level of practical (but no longer ordinary) life, and the eternal soul, the presence of God in man, on the level of eternity.

In the following sonnet death is the "intimate" (the closest or innermost) "tragedy" (suffering), an experience in which Christ is revealed as the ultimate symbol of "life in death" and as the essence of love:

151

[I manifest myself atheist in that God
should be the being of death: nor could my being
be only dried blood be; only nothingness
in contraction that vomits itself absurd.

God is the supreme Being of life
where dying is intimate tragedy
quartered and drawn by the high scream of love
with which Christ passed through the world.

From where the truth, living joy,
paradise lost in human mind
that wounds with the very light that thinks?

Christ on his cross with parted lip,
redeeming the most ancient sin,
poetry is of a pain that dies pain.]

Manifiéstome ateo de que Dios
sea el ser de la muerte: ni mi ser
sería sangre a secas; sólo nada
en contracción que se vomita absurda.

Dios es el Ser supremo de la vida
donde el morir es íntima tragedia
descuartizada por amor en grito
con el que Cristo atravesara el mundo.

¿De dónde la verdad, dicha viviente,
paraíso perdido en mente humana
que duele con la propia luz que piensa?

Cristo en su cruz con entreabierto labio,
redimiendo el pecado más antiguo,
poesía es de un dolor que al dolor muere.   (n. pag.)

"Christ crucified" in this sonnet is the ultimate symbol of
intentional suffering, the death of the body and the resurrection of the
spirit. The ancient "sin" that He cures is the "fall into separateness"
from God, the loss of consciousness of one's divine origin. Poetry for
Rielo enacts such intentional suffering--the suffering that ends

suffering. And with the death of suffering comes peace, a peace which "surpasses all understanding."

The living joy or happiness that Rielo refers to as truth is inner harmony between the emotional and intellectual centers, the congenitive unification of the "treidad." This becomes "tercio incluso"--the awakening to Third Force as the neutralizing agent that sets in motion inner creation. With regard to Rielo's insistence on such empirical mysticism, on the practical experience of awakening, it is important to note three categories of language: philosophical, theoretical, and practical. Practical language is the one requiring the most effort and it is the most useful. Philosophical language speaks on the level of possibility (and is hence non-empirical), while theoretical language remains at the generalized level of laws. In practical language, however, the scale is on one's own level, eye-to-eye so to speak, which makes it both the most useful and the most demanding form of language (Ouspensky, *Fourth Way* 341). Within this scheme, empirical mysticism may be categorized as practical language that reveals both philosophy and divine theory. Even while he draws philosophical and theoretical concerns into practical language, however, Rielo is careful not to mix these three modes of thinking. One might argue that the poetic of surrealism, placing practical language within the infrastructure of thinking in a new way, constitutes a fourth mode.

The following sonnet offers an intensely lyrical description of the ecstatic, overwhelming experience of mystical union with God. As in the classical tradition of Golden Age mystical poetry, the symbols and imagery are seemingly veiled from the eyes of the uninitiated. The imagery, however, is modern and original, and the meaning is clear to readers who have read Rielo's other poems. The dialogue form is employed, keeping everything changing, moving, in the powerful rhythm of harmonious being:

[Don't touch me, my God, don't touch me.
Already you have done it incarnate, well you know
so many flame wounds opening me saltynesses
that my death now is grave without closing

where dying dies in nameless sea,
and when it cools, my blood sticks

in the air that my *sabores*[1] breathe.
oh my soul in unbearable affliction falling in love!

Tell me, oh God, from what field am I the harvest
because it seems to me that a strong wind
is accumulating all its artists

in order that, tearing out secretly all weeds
and reducing steel into pure dust,
you might dry with steel my forged wound.]

No me toques, Dios mío, no me toques.
Ya lo has hecho encarnado, bien lo sabes,
tantas llagas abriéndome salobres
que mi muerte ya es tumba sin cerrarse

donde muriendo muere en mar sin nombre,
y cuando enfría, pégase mi sangre
en el aire que aspiran mis sabores.
¡Ay mi alma en dura pena enamorándose!

Dime, oh Dios, de qué campo soy cosecha
porque paréceme que un fuerte viento
acumulara todas sus aristas

para, arrancando oculto toda hierba
y reduciendo en puro polvo el hierro,
con hierro seques mi forjada herida.
                    (*Sombras vírgenes* n. pag.)

The fourth section of *Pasión y muerte* is introduced by two
quotations on the themes of life, death and mystic death, one from the
Bible and one from San Juan de la Cruz:

I am resurrection and the life. He who believes in me, although he
die, he will live and all who live and believe in me, never will he die.
(John 11: 25-26)

---

1.   <u>Sabores</u>: Round knobs on a horses bit.

This life that I live
is deprivation of living;
and thus, it is continual dying
until it live with you.

(San Juan de la Cruz, Vida y obras, 390)

The first poem of Rielo's in this section is called "Intemperie" ["Outdoors"]:

[Yesterday a bird moaned in my pitiful tomb.
I have left it alone with her.

Now it is hers

I am satisfied with the virginal open air
this of her--God has told me--will last me

forever, forever.]

Ayer un ave gemía en mi pobre tumba.
La he dejado con ella a solas.

Ya es de ella.

Yo me conformo con la virginal intemperie.
Esta suya --Dios me ha dicho-- me durará

siempre, siempre.

(*Pasión y muerte* 129)

By seeing one's own nothingness "my pitiful tomb", one becomes able to render the personality created by life passive, and the possibility of the development of essence emerges. Essence is that part of man inherited from the Father: "*congenitud.*" The death of which the mystic speaks is not the death of the body but rather the death of the personality that is dominated by the senses and by the influences from the material world of life. The death of personality is necessary for the development of essence--that part of man that is real, that remains impervious to the the conditioning and education of ordinary life. Essence is called the "spirit" by mystics. It is that deepest inner part of man that was sent down from a higher level, a level beyond the

155

comprehension of the finite mind. In Rielo's genetic metaphysics, development is a journey of return to that higher level, so to speak. In the Gospel of John we read:

"Verily--Verily--I say unto thee, except a man be born--Anew--from above--he cannot see the kingdom of God." Nicodemus saith unto him--How can a man be born when he is old? Can he enter a second time into his mothers womb and be born? Jesus answered--"Verily--Verily--I say unto you--except a man be born of Water and of the Spirit--he cannot enter into the Kingdom of God. That which is born of the Flesh is Flesh--and that which is born of the Spirit is Spirit. Marvel not that I said unto thee--ye must be born--anew--from Above." (John 3:5-9)

In esoteric Christianity (the hidden teachings of the New Testament) there are two kinds of suffering: the conscious and the mechanical. Mechanical suffering is the useless, habitual affliction of negative emotions, emotions which we perpetuate through all sorts of illusory justifications. This suffering stems from injuries, imagined or real, to the ego and its vanity and pride. Mechanical suffering has to be sacrificed, and, paradoxically, it is this very sacrifice that produces conscious suffering. This conscious suffering, called "suffering after a godly sort" by St. Paul,[2] leads to inner development.

Rielo, like Heidgger, points out in his philosophical writings that there can be no real justice in a world where mankind on the whole is still in a state of undeveloped conciousness or sleep and where, consequently, everything happens mechanically, in what appears to be the only way it can happen. What has been overlooked in most philosophy is that man does not possess full consciousness, although he *imagines* that he does. To suffer over "injustice" is foolish, illogical, and absolutely useless. Moreover this negative, mechanical suffering blocks the possibility of positive emotions which flow from a higher

---

2. "For though I make you sorry with my epistle, I do not regret it, though I did regret; for I see that my epistle made you sorry, though but for a season. Now I rejoice, not that ye were made sorry but that ye were made sorry after a godly sort, that ye might suffer loss by nothing. For godly sorrow worketh repentance unto salvation, a repentance which bringeth no regret: but the sorrow of the world worketh death. For behold, this self-same thing, that ye were made sorry after a godly sort, what earnest care it wrought in you, yea, what clearing of yourselves..." (II Corinthians 7:8-11)

level and do not admit of opposites. A great deal of energy is lost in negative emotions, so there is not sufficient energy remaining for anything else. Conscious suffering, then, is only experienced as suffering because one has not completely ceased to suffer mechanically. When mechanical suffering is sacrificed, a major portion of personality "dies" or becomes passive, thus the statement of the Golden Age mystic Santa Teresa: *Muero porque no muero* [I die because I do not die] (*Obras*... 499). Death and suffering are intimately related on the esoteric, mystic level where the central quest is to change one's being and consciousness. One cannot be understood without the other. The most descriptive statment of this paradox is found in the Acts of John, which is from a Gnostic book and is not usually found in the modern New Testament: "If thou hadst known how to suffer, thou wouldst have been able not to suffer. Learn thou to suffer, and thou shalt be able not to suffer" (*Secret Teachings* 59).

The sacrifice of mechanical suffering and the emergence of conscious suffering--the paradox of "pleasure in pain" as a mystical phemomenon--is a recurrent theme in Rielo's poetry. It is often related to the theme of death, understood mystically as the death of the finite self or personality of man, the self created by man's external world. One must die to the old in order for something new to be born. The effort of bringing this to pass causes pain. In Rielo's poems the juxtaposition of weeping and laughter is one of the central metaphors that symbolizes this mystical experience:

[O seal of a lip in tenacious encounter
with a shadowless love!
O clarity weeping with roses that laugh
the delicate touch of a bodyless smile!
Blue space so washed in some innocent eyes.
You, who bestow the airy volume of things;
you, who draw into your valley immense
like an immense moon or immense soul
the birds that voluptuous in your breast fall in love;
you, as toothless as the purest kiss
of a lip without sorrow, luminous, serene, beyond the weight
that a sob produces and the soul scarcely bears;
allow me to comprehend the cloud
that at this moment passes like a naked child
transferred by intangible hands.]

¡Oh sello de un labio en tenaz encuentro
con un amor sin sombras!
¡Oh claridad que llora con las rosas que ríen
el delicado tacto de una sonrisa sin cuerpo!
Espacio azul de tan lavado en unos ojos inocentes.
Tú, que otorgas el volumen airoso de las cosas;
tú, que adentras en tu valle inmenso
como inmensa luna o inmensa alma
las aves que en tu seno voluptuosas se enamoran;
tú, tan sin dientes como el beso purísimo
de un labio sin pena, luminoso, sereno, más allá del peso
que un llanto produce y el alma difícil soporta;
dame a comprender esa nube
que en este instante pasa como niño desnudo
que intangibles manos trasladan.

(*Llanto azul* 111)

The metaphor "clarity weeping with roses that laugh" becomes symbol in the context of the poet's overall system of images since "clarity," "light," and "seeing" have already been used to connote the mystic state where consciousness is changed, where one is more awake, where one perceives more light on the mental and emotional level. Clarity weeps, it suffers, but its suffering is attended by beauty (roses) and positive emotion (laughter). The notion of beauty and positive emotion as elements in the suffering of higher consciousness accords with St. Paul's idea of "godly suffering."

The second verse of this poem reads:

[Oh
no...

don't let him fall to the rootless earth
of some invalid, immobile kisses.
He's fine there. With his lip
as thin as the profile of an intact rose
or a virgin glance.
Let his flesh mature on silk
for bone is not enough...
Let him drink the density of a strong heartbeat.
Let his soul first fill blues

he will need them in his fall; and he will survive
not as a broken star, yes as deity
that pilgrim sings without astonishment.
Oh. Sing, yes, with the insistence of some fingers,
while they die, you, venerable space, will be
the sigh with which the sun gets up
after a night, serene and cold.
Yes. When the clock rings
and life begins.]

Oh
no...

no lo dejes caer en la tierra sin raíces
de unos besos inválidos, inmóviles.
Ahí está bien. Con su labio
tan fino como el perfil de una rosa intacta
o de una mirada virgen.
Dejad que madure su carne en seda
que en hueso no basta...
Dejad que tome la densidad de un latido fuerte.
Dejad que su alma primero llene azules
que en su caída le harán falta; y sobreviva
no como lucero roto, sí como deidad
que peregrina canta sin asombrarse.
Ay. Cante, sí, con la insistencia de unos dedos
que , mientras mueren, tú, venerable espacio, seas
el suspiro con que el sol se levanta
después de una noche serena y fría.
Sí. Cuando suena el reloj
y la vida empieza.

(Llanto azul 111)

In this poem as in all of Rielo's work and in the Spanish mystical
tradition generally, the kiss is symbolic of the mystic *toque* [touch].
Here the kiss, the symbol of entering into union with God, brings man
beyond the weight of suffering: "the kiss most pure." Rielo reveals in
these lines the spiritual and psychological evolution of man: the "death"
that leads to a new sense of time, a new state of being and consciousness
where man is a "pilgrim deity." Man's flesh matures by means of the

aspect of God which Rielo symbolizes as "silk." The clock striking is the active beginning of new life.

In a poem titled "Supe de Ti" ["I Knew of You"], "weeping/ sobbing," suffering in its paradoxical form, is explored in all of its aspects. The sacrifice of mechanical suffering is symbolized as the "shadow of lost sob," and conscious suffering is symbolized as "a first sob that never misses the mark." Paradoxical suffering leads to the mystic encounter of the soul with God, to change in consciousness. The "death" that constitutes the price for this encounter appears as "a kiss of whole silences falling on the hard ground of a lip." "Kiss," as always, is the symbol of union, and "lip" figures the essence of the bestower: God, the spirit (*animus*) of the soul (*anima*). In the second verse the harmonious counter-point is "a flight / in kiss" with "your lip inside," an ascent to union with the soul of the soul. The "lip" or soul of the soul is then described by means of simile as an "intangible breast that with life persists / and conquers death." Here the "death in life" of sleeping man to which St. Paul refers is the death that is conquered:

[I found out about You. Found out about You...
when your hair sharpened in lip
its magic liquid mother of pearl
in my astonishment little bird remained.
Remained to make wings of new centuries,
mine. Centuries of mine that don't allow
their continuous day to die
in the shadow of a lost sob.
I then began to live the sweet leaf
of a first sob that is never wrong.

I aspired, You know, the attempt at a flight
in kiss with your lip inside. Inside a lip
like an intangible breast that with life persists
and conquers death. Conquers, yes, furrowing a heaven
of eyeless pupil to which the modest, tender lip...

loving
subscribes.

Prisoner I remained; yes, prisoner. Or in You suspended.
Full, oh, of your lip. That whole lip

that matures laughters liquid like sobs.
Laughters that gestureless lift to the golden summit
of a naked cloud and sunny breasts
the jubilant smiling depths of a clearness
that sweetly looks at a white breath
that cannot even touch the shore
the fragile finger of the gracile bird.
I entered like that into flesh of tenuous secular heartbeats
that say its time that silence
in brilliance find what brilliance lives weeping.
Oh. The green meadow that the airs hush.]

Yo supe de Ti. Supe de Ti...
cuando tu cabello afilado en labio
su mágico líquido nácar
en mi asombro avecilla quedó.
Quedó para hacer alas de siglos nuevos,
los míos. Siglos míos que no dejan
que su día continuo pueda morir
a la sombra de un llanto perdido.
Comencé a vivir entonces la dulce hoja
de un llanto primero que nunca se equivoca.

Aspiré, Tú sabes, el intento de un vuelo
en beso con tu labio dentro. Dentro de un labio
como seno intangible que con la vida persiste
y a la muerte vence. Vence, sí, surcando un cielo
de pupila sin ojo que el pudoroso labio tierno...

              amoroso
              suscribe.

Preso quedé; sí, preso. O en Ti suspenso.
Lleno, ay, de tu labio. Ese labio entero
que madura risas líquidas como llantos.
Risas que sin gesto alzan a la dorada cima
de una nube desnuda y senos soleados
los jubilosos fondos rientes de un claro
que dulce mira un hálito blanco
que ni tocar su orilla puede
el frágil dedo de la grácil ave.

Entré así en carne de tenues latidos seculares
que dicen es tiempo de que el silencio
en el brillo halle lo que el brillo llorando vive.
Ay. El verde prado que los aires callan.   (107)

The mystics who experience higher consciousness speak of this necessary suffering, effort, and death of the personality through which one must overcome the "animal" of desire and the ego with its violence. The higher state, in other words, is not won casually by accident, or fortuitous circumstance, or luck. That is why it is often dismissed by people as imagination or speculation. Moreover, a higher state of conciousness cannot be experienced through reading or theorizing about it or examining others who have entered into it. It can only be proved directly through one's own empirical experience. Moreover, it requires tremendous effort, an effort rendered particularly difficult by the law of inertia that operates on the level of ordinary life. Everything moves downstream with the flow, but to awaken one must swim against the flow. One cannot become conscious mechanically. Therefore, one needs help and new knowledge and understanding. It is not so much that esoteric knowledge is hidden; rather, it is not wanted. The easier, softer way of "sleep" seems much more comfortable. Unfortunately, it is also much more dangerous, as we can see in our present world.

Rielo presents the reader with these ideas in his poetry, his philosophy, and his works of literary criticism. In a paper he delivered in June of 1990 in Spain titled "Dos intérpretes de la mística española en el Siglo de Oro: San Juan de la Cruz y San Ignacio de Loyola" ["Two Interpreters of Spanish Mysticism in the Golden Age: San Juan de la Cruz and San Ignacio de Loyola"], he speaks of the mystical experience of San Juan de la Cruz as an elevation to ontology. Through his own mystical experience, San Ignacio opens the road for San Juan de la Cruz and Santa Teresa de Jesus to elaborate a unitary empirical mysticism:

> Empirical mysticism ... finds its expression during the Golden Age in three peculiar forms: in San Ignacio de Loyola, the implicit spirit of the crusade; in San Juan de la Cruz, the elevation of the mystical spirit to ontology; in Santa Teresa de Jesús, the entry of mysticism into popular Castilian.... the spiritual exercise that mysticism involves has its very origin of this: the infused supernatural. Authentic mysticism implicitly contains asceticism.   ("*Dos intérpretes...*" 3)

Certain key words in this passage clarify the concepts we are analyzing in Rielo's poetry: empirical mysticism, the infused supernatural, and implicit asceticism in authentic mysticism.

The "death" of personality and the sacrifice of mechanical suffering through conscious suffering are specific objectives of asceticism. San Juan de la Cruz defines some of the particulars of the ascetic mandates:

[Let your soul therefore turn always:

Not to what is most easy, but to what is hardest;... ... ...
Not to rest, but to labor;... ... ...
Not to will anything, but to will nothing;... ... ...
To know all things, learn to know nothing.... ... ...
To learn to know nothing, go whither you are ignorant..... ..
To be what you are not, experience what you are not."
... ...
To be all things, be willing to be nothing.... ... ...
To get to where you have no taste for anything, go through whatever experiences you have no taste for.... ... ...
To reach what you possess not, go whithersoever you own nothing.... ... ...
When you stop at one thing, you cease to open yourself to the All. For to come to the All you must give up the All. And if you should attain to owning the All, you must own it desiring nothing.
... ...

In this spoliation, the soul finds tranquillity and rest. Profoundly established in the center of its own nothingness, it can be assailed by naught that comes from below; and since it no longer desires anything, what comes from above cannot depress it; for its desires alone are the causes of its woes. ("Subida del Monte Carmelo" I:13,11, *Obras*... 480-482)

In the Holy Scriptures there is also much evidence of this reversal:

Thus saith the Lord--God--"Remove the Diadem--take off the crown--exalt him that is low and abase him that is high. I will overturn--overturn--perverted--perverted--will I make it. (Ezk 21:26)

In the Oriental teachings of Buddhism, this concept is related to the divine impulse of conscience and it is said that the whole of us, the whole of our essence, is suffering because the manifestation of this impulse of conscience can only proceed from a constant struggle of two completely opposite aspects of the self.

Fernando Rielo's lyrical revelation of the implicit asceticism in mystic "death" and rebirth is presented in powerful imagery in a poem called "Sierra" from *Llanto azul*:

[Nor do they remember the past generations
that yesterday that never passes, because it never cries.
Your breeze is, beloved rock, perfumed breath
that in its rest they guard the arsenal of a kiss
powerful and fierce like the one on that day
when I, naked and pure; prisoner, Father, by your finger
on fire, grasping, ecstatic, with open arms
the unleashed storm that You brought to me.

I saw it like a host of immense horses
coming towards me; and You, riding on it
swiftly racing, volumes creating,
vomiting the majestic, flagellating rage...
I, Father, prepared my flesh for destruction.

        Oh
        yes...

Trampled on by thousands of hooves, my flesh torn to shreds
with You, Father, I wanted myself. Or, at last, for my soul
to go off enjoined... as You made it in the beginning.

        Oh!!]

Ni recuerdan siquiera las generaciones pretéritas
de aquel ayer que nunca pasa, porque nunca llora.
Tu brisa es, roca amada, perfumado aliento
que en su descanso guardan el arsenal de un beso
poderoso y bravío como el de aquel día
en que yo, desnudo y puro, preso, Padre, de tu dedo

encendido, acogiera, extático, con mis brazos abiertos
la tormenta desatada que Tú me trajiste.

Yo la vi como multitud de caballos inmensos
que a mí vinieran; y a Ti, cabalgando en ella
con veloz carrera, volúmenes creando,
vomitando el majestuoso genio flagelante...
Yo, Padre, a la destrucción mi carne dispués.

     Oh
     sí...

Pisado por miles de cascos, mi carne pedazos hecha
contigo, Padre, me quise. O, al fin, enganchada
mi alma se fuera... como Tú al principio la hiciste.

     Ay!!
         (*Llanto azul* 97)

    The key clause that reveals the esoteric meaning of change of being is *me quise* [I wanted myself]. Rielo equates the "self" he wants with his essence or soul as God made it in the beginning. Ascetic suffering is symbolized by the image of "thousands of hooves" tearing the flesh to pieces, and it is invoked explicitly in the following line (which draws on the mystical dialogue paradigm where the poetic I speaks to God directly): "I, Father, prepared my flesh for destruction." Suffering on this level is intentional or conscious suffering, not the automatic reactive suffering of injured "self-love." Conscious suffering leads to inner development.

    The great modern mystic, G. I. Gurdjieff, writes in *All and Everything* of conscious labors and intentional suffering as the only means of attaining higher states of consciousness: "endurance towards other's manifestations displeasing to oneself could alone crystallize being-parlkdolg-duty, crystallize data for the capacity of genuine being-pondering, and only this can bring awareness of genuine reality." Only by "being-parlkdolg-duty (conscious labor and intentional suffering) can "higher-being parts be coated" and sane comparative mentation and the possibillity of conscious active mentation be established. Only "higher being-bodies" functioning in their totality can actualize objective reason. Thanks to the disappearance of "being-parlkdolg-duty" man takes the ephemeral for the real, or sees reality upside down" (738).

The difference between the didactic, intellectual message of San Juan de la Cruz and the symbolic, lyrical message of Rielo illustrates an interesting point concerning the communicability of poetry in general and particularly of mystic poetry. In spite of the highly unusual, completely original, and logically difficult use of language in Rielo, the message is deeply and powerfully received by the reader on the emotional level; the cognitive aspect of the emotional center understands something new even if it cannot formulate it in the words of ordinary intellect. In contrast, the formulations of San Juan de la Cruz seem to the reader unacquainted with esoteric ideas and experiences like self- contradictions and can therefore effect no real intellectual or emotional change in that reader's understanding.

The "infused supernatural" that Rielo mentions in *"Dos intérpretes*..." is also intertwined with the themes of suffering and "death." Indeed, the very possibility of this death of the old and birth the new is founded on this concept. The essence of man originates at a higher level--the level of the stars, the Absolute or God--as opposed to the level of ordinary life from which personality springs. Thus, man is infused with the supernatural, but he is unaware of it. The renowned mystic Meister Eckhart puts it thus: "Eye wherewith I see God, that is the same eye wherewith God sees in me; my eye and God's eye, that is one eye and one vision and one knowing and one love" (206). The Scriptures also abound in references to this idea and its relationship to death and rebirth:

Yield yourselves unto God as those that are Alive from the Dead.... (Ro 6:13)

The Lord is nigh unto them that are of a broken heart and serveth such as be of a contrite Spirit. (Ps 51:17)

In a critique of *Llanto azul*, the prestigious critic Ramiro Lagos relates the concept of the infused supernatural in Rielo's poetry to revelation: "Mysticism applied to art brings us to view a poetic world in which God, as the paradigm of poetry, disseminates Himself in all His created wonders or multiples Himself in all His mirrors" (121). This mystical concept of the infused supernatural is also found in the Eastern religious teachings: In the "great dictum" of the *Upanishads*

"That art Thou," "that" means God or the Brahma, the universal source of all Being, All things being in Him. To cognize directly this "being in Him" is the mystic state, where one "dies" to oneself and experiences God as omnipotent, omnipresent and eternal. In the *Upanishads* it is explained that one who worships by thinking of the Deity as other than himself is more like an animal than a man. The mystical state is a state of being freed from the small "self," a state in which one returns to the Source. St. Paul writes: "The word of God is quick and powerful and sharper than any two-edged sword, extending even unto the sundering of the soul from the spirit." The imagery of the two-edged sword implies the cutting away of what is not absolutely real in oneself: complete reversal.

Some of the teachings involved in the effort to effect a change of being and to attain an understanding of being one with All are held in oral tradition and cannot be read about or written about. That has been true since ancient times and it remains true today. When one has sufficient understanding and preparation one receives the oral tradition: the decoding Rosetta Stone of empirical mysticism. The state of one's consciousness and being shapes one's life: when one's being has reached the level at which one may begin real efforts a teacher will be attracted and will impart this oral tradition.

In the "Now" of this movement beyond ordinary reality and ordinary time the poet *is* city or forest infused with the symbol of "silk": the soft yet empowered metaphor for God. The mystical unity is infused with life by "silken heartbeats":

[Now I am city or perhaps forest. Immense
forest of silken heartbeats
that in my love feast I long for
without complaints and without shouts, oh. Like music
of a new sun that with unpronounceable touch
tells me the happy hour of some silent eyelids
as worthy quiet monks who distil darkness.
Shaded darkness that moistened with stars
exist in sleep.]

Ya soy ciudad o acaso bosque. Bosque
inmenso de latidos sedosos
que en mi ápage ansío
sin queja y sin grito, ay. Como música
de un sol nuevo que con tacto impronunciable
me diga la feliz hora de unos párpados callados
como dignos monjes quedos que destilan oscuros.
Oscuros umbríos que mojados luceramente
en el sueño existen.

                                    (*Llanto azul* 109-110)

Rielo has become aware through his personal experience of the
presence of the divine in all the phenomena of creation, including
himself. He lives in this awareness to the fullest extent of his capacity,
keeping in mind that, as in all other states or conditions, degrees are
involved, and consciousness is also in constant flux or motion.
Consciousness is subject to the cosmic law of degrees, scale, and
change: it rises high, then ebbs back into sleep, then rises again. The
peculiar characteristic of consciousness, as compared to other natural
phenomena subject to the laws of degree, scale, and movement,
however, is that consciousness (that is, higher consciousness) can never
be automatic; it can never become an easy habit. It demands awakened
effort, a decision, determination, and striving to "be here now," to
"remember oneself." Ouspensky describes such consciousness as a
double arrow of attention, one arrow directed on oneself and the other
on the outer world or environment of the moment (*Fourth way* 115). If
you look at yourself, observe yourself in interaction, you will observe
that you are not remembering yourself in the interaction. You are
caught in the outerworld phenomenon, that is, the person you are
talking to, the thing you are doing, the show you are watching, the piece
of landscape you are admiring, etc. Your mind is rolling, your sense
organs are all functioning, but what is missing is the simultaneous
remembrance of yourself: how you are at this moment. Simply to
realize this fact, to know it from one's own experience, is a tremendous
step toward higher consciousness. It is the foundation for any possible
growth in that direction. One cannot hope to escape from prison if one
is unaware that one is in prison. It must also be noted that since to
escape from prison singlehandedly is is almost impossible, one needs
help from those who have escaped before. One may read many texts
describing these extraordinary, miraculous states, but only one's own
personal effort of self-observation, self-remembering, and
understanding, supplemented by the help of those who have already

experienced such states, can plant the mustard seed in fertile ground. Then you must also of course water it. These practical efforts are the empirical aspect of the mystic quest for union of the soul with God and change in the level of being and consciousness.

"Empirical mysticism," a fundamental theme in the writings of the Spanish mystics of the Golden Age, remains the cornerstone of the contemporary Spanish mysticism which reaches its climax in the poetry and philosophy of Fernando Rielo. Its principal tenet is that God created man for self-development, as opposed to the automatic evolution found in nature. The possibility of evolution for man lies in his consciousness and must be realized by man himself. God has placed in man the potentiating "seed" but it is man that must recognize it, nurture it and make it grow. The esoteric teaching of empirical mysticism is not intellectual theory but a lived experience that produces higher states of consciousness. The new way of thinking defined by that teaching enters the world through literature as a higher influence by means of which the reader can increase his understanding, find reinforcement in his own struggle for Being. Empirical mysticism or esoteric Christianity teaches that mankind is hypnotized or put to sleep by the powerful force of imagination; man imagines that he is fully conscious and therefore does not seek to develop further. He is imprisoned in the smallest, most dismal part of himself and does not know it. In order to get out he must somehow realize his true position.

Another parallel with the ancient teachings of esoteric Christianity can be found in the following poem from *Balcón a la bahía*:

[The lips twist quickly to devour themselves.
And they scream... scream... although it is You
walking alone upon the water.

Men only know of phantoms and death.]

Los labios se retuercen prontos a devorarse.
Y gritan... gritan... aunque seas Tú
a solas caminando sobre el agua.

Los hombres sólo saben de fantasmas y muerte.   (26)

This passage refers, of course, to the episode in which Christ goes away into the mountains near a lake. His disciples search for him in a boat out on the lake, and, when suddenly they see him coming toward them walking over the water, they are afraid, but He comforts them. Walking on water is a symbol of the effort to rise above those aspects of yourself that are bound up with ordinary life and personality: the ego asleep in negative dreams and illusion. Water, in the tradition of myth and magic, is a symbol of emotion. In Christian symbology the Heart of Jesus is bare and pierced but also draped with a gold banner representing the real heart of man from which he can perceive objective reality and conscious impartial love.

In a poem titled "*Tu paso*" ["*Your footstep*"] we read:

[Oh, memory of mine...!
When I told them
at 6 in the morning
and my dog was up at dawn:

> My friendly flowers.
> Wake up again.
> Yes. Wake up...

for death
rises from its death.
And the kisses
that never died,
await us...

> to go on
> living.]

¡Ay, memoria mía...!
Cuando yo les dije
a las 6 de la mañana
que mi perro amanecía:

> Mis flores amigas.
> Despertad de nuevo.
> Sí. Despertad...

que la muerte
de su muerte resucita
Y los besos
que nunca murieron,
nos esperan...

para seguir
viviendo.
(*Llanto azul* 36)

And in the book of verse called *Pasión y muerte* we read:

[Death, oh, is only the riverbank
of two worlds that embrace.]

La muerte, ay es solo orilla
de dos mundos que se abrazan.   (63)

[Death--a voice told me--in itself is nothing.
It happens that men hate her...

and that is why they build tombs.

Life, oh, does not end with any death,
because nothing exists that infringes upon its destiny.

Everything that it is... will keep on being.]

La muerte--una voz me dijo--en sí no es nada.
Sucede que los hombres la odian...

y por eso levantan sepulcros.

La vida, ay, no acaba con ninguna muerte,
porque nada existe que infrinja su destino.

Todo lo que es... seguirá siendo.   (84)

The very title of this volume--*Pasión y muerte*, [Passion and death]--reveals the relation between its two terms as that of *definiens* and *definiendum*: passion defines death, death defines passion (7).

López Sevillano points out that when the Third Force is constituted by ordinary life or things of the exterior, material world, man remains as he is; no change can occur. The First Force or active force meets always in life with Second Force or passive and denying force. For any real change to take place, something new must enter: Third Force as originating in Higher Mind. This cosmic law emanates through all worlds. If Third Force originates in higher mind, inner development can occur. This is the *tercio incluso* of Rielo's metaphysics literally translated: the "third included".

Although a reader imprisoned in ordinary states of consciousness might see Rielo's poems as semi-tragic, they are from the mystical perspective profoundly optimistic. The aesthetic intensity of Rielo's poetry stems from the poet's direct inspiration by objective reality, an inspiration that suffuses his aesthetically evocative poetic language. The magnitude of Rielo's achievement as a poet can be measured by his capacity of empowerment in the poem. One of the key words in the prologue to *Pasión y muerte* is *"intencionalidad"* ["intentionality"]:

> The characteristic of mystic poetry is precisely that celestial vision from which it is illuminated, in this case, the significance of life and death, is the science of intentionality specifically transcendental, the incitation of the Divine. (López Sevillano, "Prologue" 7)

This incitation of intentionality toward the divine begins with the meditative state where thought is quieted and efforts are made to focus sensuous attention in the whole of the body and to focus emotional attention in the feeling of conscious presence of the whole of the self. In the *Poe'S* God becomes an aesthetic expression: God as landscape of the soul. "Being," suffused by the *tercio incluso*, fills the formalities and specifics of the language of poetry with trascendental content. The potentiating force of these linguistic forms, in other words, comes from the *tercio incluso*, the infused Third Force which is the balancing or neutralizing force of higher mind, the force that leads to a new understanding and a new level of being.

Rielo's words go whirling into all hearts, whispering, "Come with peace." With conscious love he comes as a poet, a mystic, and a modern hero, bringing his message of peace of heart, content to trust his own given heritage of life. He calls on mankind to detect that gleam of power in itself, a light of dearly bought intelligence giving color to human existence. Rielo's life work bears rich fruit for many: the evolution of the individual; the goal of making all mankind one, each individual taking responsibility for those around him. Rielo's presence is a rhythm of a universal heartbeat--pulsating harmonies that are the sound of celestial music.

Destiny
As Time And Immortality

"When the doors of perception Are clean, everything is *seen* as it is: Infinite and Eternal."
>   --William Blake

"I know that whatsoever God doeth it shall be done forever: nothing can be put to it nor anything taken away from it." (Ec 3:14)

Rielian mysticism reveals dimensions of time beyond the senses. The senses can only perceive time in the present moment. Past and future time do not exist for the senses; rather, the past exists in memory and the future in imagination. However, we are not fully conscious in the present moment in spite of this. Conciousness is not part of the senses; it functions apart from them, above them, so to speak. Somehow, consciousness brings memory and imagination together and thus keeps one outside of the present moment. Thus there is disharmony between the senses and consciousness. The mystic state revealed by Rielo in his poetry, however, unites both the senses and consciousness in the present moment. The "now" is thus elevated to a moment in eternity as well as in time. Eternity penetrates moving time in the present moment. The full consciousness of "now," pervading the whole of the self, inspires a feeling of eternity, a positive emotion. That full consciousness is always available if we will only make the effort to enter into it. To be before the present moment in memory, or after the present moment in dreams or imagination of the future is to be absent from the "now" in consciousness. The senses, which can only register the present moment, are not balanced; they are not working with full consciousness. The mystic state requires attention and awareness to the sacred "temple"--the body--and thus brings the different aspects of man's functions into harmony. The entry of eternity into time occurs when this harmony is produced. The mystic symbol of this esoteric idea is the cross: the vertical line is the line of eternity; the horizontal line is ordinary time moving from past to future; the meeting point in the cross is the "eternal now," a now that always "is" in life, though we may not be conscious of it. Thus man lives in eternity, but in his ordinary state of consciousness he cannot sense this. One example (among the many we find in Rielo's verse) of the feeling of eternity in time appears in the following poem from *Dios y árbol*:

> [Now I will not cede the valley
> my celestial state
>
> I promise you.
>
> That is why I have my rib open
> through which passes time...
>
>   without complaining.]

> Ya no cederé al valle
> mi celeste estadio.
>
> Te lo prometo.
>
> Para eso tengo mi costado abierto
> por donde pasa el tiempo...
>
>   sin quejarse.   (88)

Another example appears in the poem "Tiempo no es cuándo" ["Time Is Not When"] from *Noche clara*:

> [I have arrived on time.
> I have arrived on time.
> I have arrived at the origin of time
>
> When time is not yet when.
> When it begins to be moment
> of a first tear that jumps
> and in the act it trembles.

175

And runs, runs... with feeling of the universe.
a universe that seems never to end.
Universe that is the step with which you walk,

with which you walk...
with your sob on high...]

He llegado a tiempo.
He llegado a tiempo.
He llegado al origen del tiempo.

Cuando tiempo no es cuándo todavía.
Cuando empieza a ser momento
de una primera lágrima que salta
y en el acto se estremece.

Y corre, corre... con sentido de universo.
Un universo que parece nunca acaba.
Universo que es el paso con que tú andas,

con que tú andas...
con tu llanto a cuestas.   (72)

Commenting on this poem in an introductory note, the noted hispanist Hugo Petraglia Aguirre states: "The origin of time is 'God Himself,' the sole container, incommensurable principle of principles according to the Evangelism of San Juan. And to arrive at the origin of time is "to be" not only as contemplator and witness, but even more, to rise to the transcendent essence of the Absolute" (13).

In a poem titled "Hora" ["Hour"] from the volume *Paisaje desnudo* we read:

[Hour is not time defined
            that can enclose itself in my bedroom clock

... ...
The soul has its exact hour
            only one.

This hour never passes,
            always it is the same.
... ...
Oh indivisible time, unique,
            insaciable hour that never goes out...
                        if you inhabit it.]

Hora no es tiempo definido
            que pueda encerrar en mi reloj de alcoba.

... ...
El alma tiene su hora exacta,
            sólo una.

Esta hora no pasa nunca,
            siempre es la misma.

... ...
Oh tiempo indivisible, único,
            hora insaciable que nunca se apaga...
                        si tú la habitas.   (95-96)

The eternal in man, his eternal life, transcends time. The temporal dimension of the senses lacks the perspective of scale and levels. On a higher level where the whole is seen, past, present, and future all appear as a unit. Thus "now" is involved in both past and future. The past is not gone forever, although our senses and reason on the ordinary level of consciousness might persuade us so. Higher dimensions are sensed by internal, not external, faculties. Thus in Santa Teresa we see the *castillo interior* [internal castle] where the search for higher dimensions takes place. This castle is the invisible world within man which he must enter if he is to experience eternity. This inner part of man--the soul or essence which Rielo describes in his philosophy as *congenitud*--is itself eternal, and it is only this part of man's being that can sense eternal time. In Rielo we read:

[It happens with time that it passes.
That it passes and it remains.

Its gesture is, oh is, like an open hand
quick to fall.

That which no one wants.
And nevertheless... she lights a fire
which no one can put out.]

Sucede con el tiempo que pasa.
Que pasa y queda.

Su gesto es, ay, como una mano abierta
pronto a derribarse.

Lo que nadie quiere.
Y sin embargo... ella enciende
lo que nadie apaga.

(*Dios y árbol* 115)

Ordinary time is external, a function of the lower influences of material life. When man reasons from ordinary time, his understanding is limited and his knowledge of himself and his position as part of the whole is erroneous. He does not "know himself"; his origin and his destiny are seen only "through a glass darkly." All mystical experience, in contrast, has in it the quality of eternity--the "fire / which no one can put out." Through such experience, personality is overcome. The desire for the things of ordinary life, the animal passions and the ego are made passive, made to "die," so that the innermost man can make contact with his ultimate source, his origin: God.

In a poem titled "Espíritu amante" ["Loving Spirit"] from *Paisaje desnudo,* man's essence is described as "loving spirit"; the sense of eternity and the necessity of the death in life of the personality are both expressed with vivid lyrical imagery:

[You have given me, Father, your loving spirit
and it is perhaps, because of this, that my kiss
and my lips endure half-opened.
Attentive to You trembling, almost motionless,
with all their breath ready without further labor
that maintains itself... for a journey so long,
where death plays so important a role.

And then?
Then exists...

Is it not perhaps then the brief instant that endures
when the last spring, enters within me
and comfortably seats itself on my first kiss

       with right of passage?

Oh long, eternal, journey, when they are no longer skys
which you contemplate nor even feelings
and if the smile of an essence...

       Let it perfume all!]

Tú me has dado, Padre, tu expíritu amante
y es quizá, por eso, que mi beso se insomnie
y mis labios perduren entreabiertos.
Atentos a Tí, trémulos, casi sin movimiento,
con todo su aliento dispuesto sin más trabajo
que contenerse... para un viaje tan largo,
donde la muerte juega un papel tan importante.

¿Y luego?
Luego existe...

¿No es acaso luego el breve instante que dura
cuando primavera, la última, me entre dentro
y cómoda se siente en mi beso de primera

       con derecho a paisaje...?

¡Oh largo, eterno, viaje, cuando ya no son cielos
lo que contemplas ni siquiera sentimientos
y sí la sonrisa de una esencia...

       que todo lo perfuma!   (113)

    The mystic experience, the change of being, is a change from lower
to higher, an entrance into a realm where time is alive in the whole:
past, present, and future:

[I am dawn in You
every day, every instant.

I know it when transposed I remain.
when I do not know if I have died...

or I have lived eternally.]

Yo soy amanecer en Ti
cada día, cada instante.

Lo sé cuando traspuesto me quedo.
Cuando no sé si he muerto...

o eternamente he vivido.
(*Pasión y muerte* 105)

This new understanding changes entirely the perception of "self":

[What can you tell me of time then...?
To what can you invite me
you who did not give me a soul, this soul
that weeps me in the measure that it learns...?

Oh, march on, centuries, march on!
I am something else.

That... which only God comprehends.]

¿Qué puede decirme el tiempo entonces...?
A qué puede invitarme
quien no me dio el alma, esta alma
que me llora a medida que aprende...?

¡Oh, marchaos, siglos, marchaos!
Yo soy otra cosa.

Eso... que sólo Dios comprende.
(*Paisaje desnudo* 118)

In San Juan de la Cruz "self" becomes God and God becomes "self." Rielian metaphysics calls this new self-perception the deity and attributes its emergence in man to the Third Force changing from the ordinary life forces of the material world to the influence of the teachings of Christ. Eternal life is found at this level. Death and life form a repeating circle in this dimension where life is always victorious. That part of man "inherited genetically" from a higher level, God, lives again and again. However, the question is: if that part is not developed, but covered over by the mechanical forces of life that man refuses to separate from (ego, vanity, pride, envy, hatred and violence), what becomes of it? There is no "something for nothing" in the sacred laws that govern self-development and higher consciousness in man. The repeated symbol of necessary suffering in the mystic writings bears witness to this fact. Christ crucified is the ultimate symbol of the necessity of intentional suffering in esoteric Christianity.

Our origin lies not in the realm of earth and time, but rather in a higher, invisible realm, a realm incomprehensible to ordinary mind. The ascetic practice and exercise of the mystic bring a new understanding, an idea of higher mind, the light of consciousness. To become something new, the old must first be done away with. Payment must be made in advance. The world as we see it from the limited perspective of the mind of the senses must be seen as unreal, as illusion. This realization carries inherent struggle. If one does not suffer and struggle with what is lower in himself, essence or soul cannot develop.

A passage from San Juan de la Cruz that introduces the third section of *Paisaje desnudo* reads:

[Oh soft hand! Oh delicate touch,
that tastes of eternal life,
and all debt pays!
Killing, you have changed death into life.]

¡Oh mano blanda! ¡Oh toque delicado,
que a vida eterna sabe,
y toda deuda paga!
Matando, muerte en vida la has trocado.
                              (Canciones del alma 111,2)

This passage is followed immediately by the voice of Christ:

"If one wishes to follow me, he must deny himself, take up his cross and follow me. Because he who would save his life will lose it, but he who loses his life for me, will find it." (Mt 6:24)

Rielo in a poem calls this salvation through loss of life "*muerte atenta*" ["attentive death"]:

[Death accompanying me
            always attentive.

She, oh, informs me
            of the passage of birds.

Of her exact hour.

Because of that they leave me the wake
            of her loving wing...

> that I gather
> every morning.]

La muerte me acompaña
            siempre atenta.

Ella, ay, me informa
            del paso de la aves.

De su hora exacta.

Por eso me dejan la estela
            de su ala amante...

> que yo recojo
> cada mañana.

(Pasión y muerte 95)

The historical documentation on Spanish mysticism conclusively demonstrates that the hermetical movement had considerable influence. In an ancient text *Hermetica* we read:

God makes the Aeon, the Aeon makes the kosmos, the kosmos makes time, and time makes coming-to-be. The essence of God is the Good, the essence of Aeon is sameness, the essence of the kosmos is order, the essence of time is change, and the essense of coming-to-be is life. The workings of God are mind and soul, the workings of the Aeon are immortality and duration, the workings of the kosmos are re-instatement in identity and re-instatement by substitution, the workings of time are increase and decrease, and the workings of coming-to-be are quality and quantity. The Aeon then is in god, the kosmos is in the Aeon, time in the kosmos, and coming-to-be takes place in time. (1:221)

The pattern of existence is presented here as a set of concentric circles, one lying inside the other. This pattern reveals the principle of scale--a hierarchy. In the *Hermetica* the following exercise is found:

Think that you are not yet begotten, think that you are in the womb, that you are young, that you are old, that you are dead, that you are in the world beyond the grave, grasp all that in your thought at once, all times and all places." (1:22)

According to this ancient text, the only way God can be perceived is to lift oneself out of the world of the senses into the realm of higher ideas where time and space are seen as a whole--past, future, and the "now" extended into a new dimension of perception. Sensual thought cannot reveal God or the already existing higher levels of ourselves that lie in our essence or soul. When this higher level of the self is freed from the bondage of the material world of the senses, the illusion of "passing time" is erased and real time in eternity is sensed. Distinctions between yesterday, today, and tomorrow no longer exist. In the mystic state, God is always everywhere, and the soul united with God, its consciousness expanded, feels the magnitude of His presence. The invisible side of oneself and existence becomes real. Consciousness is changed in quality not quantity, like the metamorphosis of caterpillar into butterfly. Its very nature changes or evolves. Developed consciousness is more than expanded awareness; it is a "different" awareness. The sadness of things as "dead and gone" in the world is transformed to a positive emotion of the miraculous nature of life. Ecstatic joy is the new emotion that replaces melancholy and sadness. The Scriptures reveal this in the notion of God as the Alpha and Omega, the beginning and end of all.

Discussing the volume *Pasión y muerte*, López Sevillano writes:

It is the reality of the lived sob by the poet that defines the terms of his poetry; through these, with his semantic fields of value, he expresses the distinct aspects of his mystic experience, one of these aspects in clarified in *Passion and Death*. ("Prologue" 5)

The negative concept of death as separation of the soul and the body, as the ending of life is absent in the poems from this volume. Death is elevated to a moment where there is no time, where time is encompassed in eternity. Death becomes the shore of two worlds embracing:

[Death, oh, is only the riverbank
of two worlds that embrace.]

La muerte, ay, es sólo orilla
de dos mundos que se abrazan.
                    (*Pasión y muerte* 63)

In the introduction to the French translation of Rielo's *Dios y árbol* (*Dieu et arbre*), Claude Couffon writes:

"En France, nous le savons, une telle attitude a inspiré Chateaubriand dans son Génie du Christianisme. Avec faste, avec magnificence, avec peut-être trop de solennité. Chez Fernando Rielo, on le sent dès le premier contact avec *Dieu et Arbre*, la quete est plus modeste, elle se fait dan la contemplation certes, mais plus discrètement: dan l'observation des choses quotidiennes, dans l'intimité que chaque etre humain a avec ceux et ce qui l'entoure..." (7).

In "Cuando vienes" ["When You Come"], Rielo's lyrical description of the unifying, all-encompassing essence of God is revealed. The poet and the phenomena observed are as one and the same; all of nature blends in eternal time, which is described as an "instant." Walking silk is the modern Rielian version of the symbolic Biblical image of walking on the water. But here the mystical language of "unification" brings silk also into the absolute act of walking. Hence the paradoxical "traspasándose" ["self-surpassing"] in language by which the doer becomes both his action and its object, as in Derridian *differAnce*:

[When you come like walking silk
with your cedar of sea foam and bird smile;
when the most secret kiss is deep
in the sea-like days of my blood.
I hear dance with her loud cry
the virgin destiny of a breast in oval
that in the heart beat the fields sings.
Freed forever from a shinning that never rests.

In that moment...

Moment of musical breezes
that playful and juicy play with all the sounds
of green and rose--sounds that exist
because they laugh--at a kiss that doesn't run away
and its footstep never ceases. Yes my laughter
I hide in the root of a endless tree
that in sap or blood the vein runs.]

Cuando vienes como seda caminante
con tu cedro de espuma y sonrisa de ave;
cuando el beso secretísimo es hondo
en los días marinos de mi sangre,
oigo cómo danza con el llanto
el virgen destino de un seno en óvalo
que en el latido canta los campos
desprendidos de un brillo que nunca descansa.

En ese instante...

Instante de musicales brisas
que jugosas juegan con todos los tonos
del verde y del rosa--tonos que existen
porque ríen--a un beso que no huye
y su paso no cede. Sí mi risa
escondo en la raíz de un árbol continuo
en que savia o sangre la vena recorre.
                              (*Llanto azul* 109)

From the point of view of the sexological analysis of language, it
appears that, in this poem, masculine nouns are feminized by means of

pure-symbol. The pure-symbol of "virginity," for example, changes the sex of the masculine noun *el destino* to *la destina*, since the term "virgin" has historically referred primarily to females. The importance of the symbol "virgin" must be emphasized. Even destiny is "virgin" in this poem, which suggests that the theme of the poem itself is virginity--the sex force brought under the light of conscious attention and transmuted into energy of a very special quality that gives additional force for the power to make conscious effort. The vow of chastity taken by priests and initiates throughout history testifies to the empirical experience of this sacrifice. That vow enables sex force to become the exchanging of energy. Transmuted into its highest finest form, sex force gives man easier access to objective reason and impartial love. This concept is not theory to Rielo but an empirical practice of absolute celibacy and a renewal of that vow on a weekly basis. This high spiritual standard is the norm of all *Idente* missionaries, male and female. The symbolic mystical model of the virgin is *La Santísima Virgen* [the Blessed Virgin]: the extended symbol of the heavenly creative power that does not need the animal passion placed in man for procreation, the power of the law that makes three into one. The image of the dove is often closely related to Mariology, while a bird inverted represents Third Force, the Holy Spirit.

Rielo's pure-poetry, as López Sevillano puts it, is "instant and instantaneously eternal. Thus in his poems physical days passing and past [*transcurridos*] are centuries and at the same time moments not lived on this earth, aesthetically intemporal" (López Sevillano, "Prologue", *Paisaje desnudo* 9-10):

[Forgotten friend of guesses
forgive the voice "moment"
in my poor verse insisting.
It is because they have been moments,
embroidered one upon the other like the feathers
of a wing, lifted in flight,
they have made me witness of entire universes....]

Amigo de adivinaciones ignotas...
perdona que la voz "instante"
en mis pobres versos se insista.
Se debe a que han sido instantes,

bordados unos a otros, como las plumas
de un ala, que alzada en vuelo,
me han hecho testigo de universos enteros...
(Llanto azul 43)

Immortality, the eternal in all that is, is blended in Rielo with the symbols of the mystic encounter: the kiss, the lip, the soul, wings. In the poem "Alzate" ["Rise up"] we read:

[When my eyes were not the loving furrow
that with lip passion writes,
my voice already was the crying of the day
Bitter day that sweetly seals the aroma of a wing
that is never extinguished, that eternal whispers,
Clear day that never confuses
the sweet star with sweet cry.
Neither does the multitude of lips
zephyrs get delirious on the lovely countenence...

      kisses.

Kisses, yes, that bright and shinning dream
in tranquil skys. Skys, oh,
that before blues live
a lip is born and its sweet singing trill.
Since then... my loving passion
traverses voices; and to choirs ascending,
hymns creates that perfume heaven.

Oh
passion,

run, fly, be carried out of yourself... And in the air
suspending... you are still nest.
In this way. Like a sobless sob,
changed into feathers.

Shout Oh passion your gracile silences
like child's fingers to the master of birds.
He knows... that in his lip live
thicknesses of wings
like sweet pine groves.]

187

Cuando mis ojos no eran el surco amoroso
que con labio la pasión escribe,
mi voz ya era el llorar del día.
Agrio día que dulce sella el aroma de un ala
que nunca se apaga, que eterna murmura.
Día claro que nunca confunde
la dulce estrella con el dulce lloro.
Tampoco la multitud de labios
que céfiros deliran en el bello gesto...

　　　　　　besos.

Besos, sí, que lúcidos sueñan
en cielos tranquilos. Cielos, ay,
que antes que azules vivan
nace un labio y su dulce trino.
De entonces... mi pasión amante
voces recorre; y a coros subiendo,
himnos crea que el cielo perfuman.

Oh
pasión,

corre, vuela, ráptate...Y en el aire
suspensa... nido te quedes.
Así. Como un llanto sin llanto,
convertido en plumas.

Grita oh pasión tus silencios gráciles
como dedos de niño al maestro de aves.
Sabe... que en su labio viven
espesuras de alas
como dulces pinares.　　(103)

In the mystic experience, ordinary time disappears; there is no yesterday of memory, no projection of past into tomorrow. A new sense of time emerges: the "eternal now" apprehended by direct cognition. Eternity enters into time, and it is in time that all movement takes place. Eternity is not limited by the conditions of time, and time is eternal in virtue of its cyclic recurrence. The mystic's moment of truth, the place where he stands to face his destiny, is absolutely new. It is not the standpoint of the ordinary feeling of oneself, the narrow view of reality conditioned by the ordinary form of our perception. Rather, the transforming power of the mystic's state of being, conciousness, and presence changes the sense of reality and also the sense of time. Beyond ideas is the eternal now, what Rielo calls the "astonishing moment." To be in this present moment is to see what one does not see: "Ahora veo lo que no veo" [Now I see what I do not see.] (*Balcón a la bahía* 40)

Rielo writes:

[Who remembers the origins of the ancient dream,
the great revelation of the angel with sword?
One makes oneself more god proportionately with more
                                         dying.]

¿Quién recuerda el origen del antiguo sueño,
la gran revelación del ángel con espada?
Hácese uno más dios cuanto más muere.   (60)

Destiny
As Conscious Love

"Set me as a seal upon thine heart, as a seal upon thine arm; For love *is* strong as death."

(Song of Solomon 8:6)

At a level of higher Being, real conscience is developed and becomes the basis of actions towards others. The lower animal aspect of man is permanently overcome. This possibility is a "grace" given by God in Rielian mystical symbology wherein the lower aspects of man--vanity, egoism, and self--are no longer given expression. This state is only reached, according to Rielian metaphysics, through asceticism, struggle, and effort. In this state, man is freed from his chains; he is liberated.

The ascetic practice of "dying to oneself" and "intentional suffering" leads to inward development of essence. This practice is a transformational process where the impressions of the self and the intellectual, emotional, and sexual-instinctual centers merge and become balanced, blending their energies in the creative, poetic act of communication of a new level of conscience. Rielo's perspective of conscious love is best expressed by himself. In one of his sonnets he writes:

[Humbleness cell of love, when will your door be opened?
Look, Father, how hushed: nothing of anything is said.
Only your meager window in front of the wall of my garden.
"Make it a sister, son, the love that I made into a golden key."

Humbleness soft caress of love is dart that certifies
Oh cherub reverberating my mind that crystalizes
idea of You who loves you deeply, never stiff idea of You.
Free me from believing that only to think you my soul might redeem

the majesty of creating me as an image of your life.
If I have your greatness, how many miseries do I not leave behind?
Oh, not one sings, all weep wounded love.

I am soul in fogless hour that from climb to climb,
on the height of heights unleafing me in me I distance myself
Make my being forgotten in my nothingness be grasped by You.]

Humildad celda de amor ¿cuándo se abrirá tu puerta?
Mira, Padre, qué callado: nada de nada se dice.
Sólo tu escasa ventana frente al muro de mi huerta.
"Hermánala, hijo, al amor que llave de oro la hice."

Humildad suave caricia de amor es dardo que acierta.
Oh querube traspasando mi mente que cristalice
idea de Ti que te adore, nunca de Ti idea yerta.
Líbrame de creer que sólo pensarte mi alma amortice

la grandeza de crearme para imagen de tu vida.
Si grandeza tengo tuya ¿cuántas miserias no dejo?
Ay, ninguna canta, todas lloran el amor herido.

Soy alma en hora sin bruma que de subida en subida,
de alto en alto deshojándose, de mí en mí yo me alejo
Haz que olvidado en mi nada mi ser quede por Ti asido.
                                    (*Sombras vírgenes* n. pag.)

The process or technique of deconstruction as defined by Jacques
Derridá in "White Mythology" is seen in Rielo's technique of

transposing by "naming" or "signifying." The Derridian "signified" is transmuted by the modifiers or adjectives in the pure-symbol through "dialogue," already established lexically, at the level of higher Being. Thus the symbol "Humbleness soft caress" at the ordinary level of reference is constituted through the modification of "Humbleness" by the metaphorically descriptive signifiers "caress" and "soft." At the esoteric, mystical level of reference, however, the signifier is united inextricably with the signified. When the two levels are in harmonious balance, the law of the Third Force or *tercio incluso* comes into play as impartial love: "the cross of Christ" as poetical, lyrical, pure-symbol.

Ancient mythological sculpture incorporates techniques that would later be adopted by surrealism. One sculpture, for example, places the breasts of a virgin (in bronze) at the head of the represented figure in order to symbolize thinking (a function of the head) with the heart (found within the breast). The neck of this sculpture is made of pure amber, which mythically is a very special form of matter that reunites and divides the three aspects of the substance of life. The amber functions as a filter upward and downward to insure impartial love and awakened intelligence. The "body" of this mythical sculpture is a bull, symbolic in the animal kingdom of the strongest physical body: signifier of the great strength needed in the spiritual quest. The legs are the legs of a lion, the most courageous of all animals, signifier of the courage required to spring forth. Finally, this sculpture has the wings of an eagle, the highest soaring bird, signifier of the necessity of flying high in thought above the desires of the body and the material world. (Gurdjieff)

In the following sonnet the poet presents the mystical communication of conscious, impartial love:

[Love is divine tear that consumes
my excellent[3] eye of living: now I hardly have eye.
I cry you, love, within, within I offer suffering.
Am I not of your tree new root of its perfume?

---

3. I use "excellent" as an equivalent for "olmo", meaning digno de veneración (worthy of veneration), as with the saints; the word implies a tremendous and sacred sense of respect. It also relates to vivificar, vivificador (making something more alive). It is an ancient Spanish word.

My soul with my soul on high, tired my soul, submerges
my soul in my soul, soul, all soul with hands full
of iron rod[4] passion that breaks my chains
and my soul, always my soul, soul with you overwhelms

the siege of the devil with grace that is born,
the claw of the howl of steel love,
for the unrepentant[5] weight for the weight that remakes

the wound with its wound[6]: deaths that in deaths I die,
deaths of deaths, death that in death is untied.
Be now your love for me, love that I eteral love!]

El amor es divina lágrima que consume
mi almo ojo del vivir: ya no tengo ojo apenas.
Te lloro, amor, por dentro, por dentro dono penas.
¿No soy de tu árbol nueva raíz de su perfume?

Mi alma con mi alma a cuestas, cansada mi alma, sume
a mi alma en mi alma, alma, todo alma a manos llenas
de almádena pasión que rompa mis cadenas
y mi alma, siempre mi alma, alma contigo abrume

el asedio del diablo por la gracia que nace,
la garra del gemido por el amor de acero,
el pesar incontrito por el pesar que rehace

la herida con su llaga: muertes que en muertes muero,
muertes de muertes, muerte que en muerte desenlace.
¡Séame ya tu querer, querer que eterno quiero!

(Sombras vírgenes n. pag.)

---

4. "Iron rod" is my equivalent for "almádena," un mazo de hierro (a stick made of
    iron used to break stones).

5. "Unrepentant" is my equivalent for "incontrito," impenitente, no se arrepiente
    (making no penance, no sacrifice, no repenting)

6. "Wound" is my equivalent for llaga; this word, which may also mean "ulcer" or
    "sore," is an ancient mystical symbol and, in Spanish mystical texts, is frequently
    combined by alliteration with the word llama (flame), referring to the flame of
    purification or conscious suffering.

The law of three--"the law of the higher blending with the lower to actualize the middle"--reveals the unlimited power from God which produces healing (Petacchi 5). All such power is void of the self-love of the ego and is instead characterized by some form of impartial love. Christ had the being of a sacred man guided by a higher order of laws. Such a man is not dominated by the impulses of greed and hate, but rather expresses the impulses of hope and of love:

[Oh Christ, my Word, how many passing
rivers of my passion quickly circling,
rivers of sob prompt wounds
my blood with your blood maturing go.

Polishing my crucified loves
now my cross of your cross embrace is kissing
our dying to live in love with each other.
We are children of the same Father burning

the tick-tock of a clock with its sad time
Your time in You passed... in suffering mine remains
to go from sky to sky to the sky that You are.

Love, lifted love, your love that you gave me
is our love far from all path.
Oh Christ that with loves arrow you wound me!]

Oh Cristo, Verbo mío, cuántos pasados
ríos de mi pasión veloces rodando,
ríos de llanto presuroso llagados
van mi sangre con tu sangre madurando.

Puliendo mis amores crucificados
ya mi cruz de tu cruz abrazo es besando
nuestro muriendo vivir enamorados.
Somos hijos de un mismo Padre quemando

el tictac de un reloj con su tiempo triste.
Tu tiempo en Ti pasó... en pena el mío queda
para ir de cielo en cielo al cielo que Tú eres.

Amor, subido amor, tu amor que me diste
es nuestro amor lejos de toda vereda.
¡Oh Cristo que con dardo de amor me hieres!

(Sombras vírgenes n. pag.)

With respect to the theme of conscious love represented in the figure of Christ, Rielo's verse can be paralleled with that of José García Nieto. Rosario Hiriart in her excellent work on Nieto, *La mirada poética de José García Nieto*, analyses this aspect in detail. She points out the clear and very personal presence of God in his poems, and the desire to identify the self with Him. (47) Nietos poem titled "En la ermita de Cristo de Gracia" [In the hermitage of Christ of Grace], Grace is the symbol of compassionate, tender conscious love:

[To be a wing
lost, Christ of Grace,
knocking in flight
at the crystal of your windows.

Or to be in the hard marble
water with your water name.

Or shivering metal
of your singular bell.

Oh child, Lord, playing
--having you and without thinking you--
at the entrance hall of your house.

Or hand raising the white
form of your dead body
with the dawn.]

Ser un ala
perdida, Cristo de Gracia,
para llamar en un vuelo
al cristal de tus ventanas.

O ser en el duro mármol
agua con tu nombre agua.

195

O metal estremecido
de tu única campana.

Oh niño, Señor, jugando
--teniéndote y sin pensarte--
en el atrio de tu casa.

O mano alzando la blanca
forma de tu cuerpo muerto
con el alba.

(Del Campo y Soledad 17)

The almost mystic desire for unification noted by Hiriart is not the only element which clearly marks the similarities between Rielo and Nieto in poetic theme and use of symbol (Nieto won the Fernando Rielo Prize for mystic poetry in 1987). The monologue-dialogue between God and poet is another, as are the symbols of the wing, the crystal, Christ, the mixing of light and "the beginning" with death, as in the lines *cuerpo muerto / con el alba* [body dead / with the dawn].

Another beautiful poem by Nieto that also reveals many similarities between these two great poets is the following:

[How quiet the world is now. And you, my God
how near you are. I could even touch you
an even recognize you in any part
of the world. I could say: river,
and name your blood. In the empty space
of this afternoon, say: God, and find you
in those clouds. Oh Lord, speak to you
and belong to you in this verse of mine!
because you are so in everything, and I feel it
that, more than ever, in the quietude of the day
your hands and your accent reveal themselves.
I would say death, now, and it would not be heard
my voice. Eternity, it would repeat
the ancient and musical tongue of the wind.]

Qué quieto está ahora el mundo. Y tú, Dios mío,
qué cerca estás. Podría hasta tocarte.
Y hasta reconocerte en cualquier parte
de la tierra. Podría decir: río,

y nombrar a tu sangre. En el vacío
de esta tarde, decir: Dios, y encontrarte
en esas nubes. ¡Oh señor, hablarte,
y responderme tú en el verso mío!
porque estás tan en todo, y yo lo siento,
que, más que nunca, en la quietud del día
se evidencian tus manos y tu acento.
Diría muerte, ahora, y no se oiría
mi voz. Eternidad, repetiría
la antigua y musical lengua del viento.

> (Nieto, Las mil mejores... 717)

This theme of "conscious love" is the center of gravity or magnetic center of the modern renaissance of spiritual poetry in the mystical tradition. There are many modern peninsular poets with poems that fall within this framework: Blanca Andreu, Jorge Justo Padron, María Victoria Atencia, Clara Janés, Ana María Fagundo, Ana María Navales, Pilar Paz, and Odón Betanzos, among others. One of the unifying sources of this new movement in Spanish poetry is the great nineteenth-century German Romantic poet Rainer María Rilke, who speaks of conscious love in his "Letters to Merline":

[Love acted on me by means of provocations, to the point where I attempted to place myself through the ecstatic eye the desired fruit, as if the eye were mouth; fruit it was, so I assure you.] (57)

Juan Ramón Jiménez is another important relatively recent Spanish source for mystical themes, though one should also note the crucial contributions of Gerardo Diego, who passed away only a few years ago, and of Camilo José Cela.

In his brilliant study *Diez años de poesía española (1960-1970)* [Ten Years of Spanish Poetry (1960-1970)], José Olivio Jiménez confirms the emergence of a new spiritual momentum among the modern poets of Spain. Speaking of Carlos Busoño, he defines Busono's principal theme as "the search for a transcendental basis conceivable even in the river-beds, so to speak, of traditional religion" (Jiménez). These river-beds (cauces) are indeed the source of contemporary mystical poetry in Spain.

One can also trace the abundant influence of Spanish mysticism in literary works from Latin America and other parts of the

197

Spanish-speaking world, as in the "mythical" poetry of Carlos Castañeda, poetry that is mixed into larger prose works and spoken in this instance by a character named Silvio Manuel:

> [I gave myself already to the power that rules my destiny.
> I do not cling now to anything so that thus to have nothing to
> defend.
> I have no thoughts, so that thus to be able *to see*.
> I fear nothing, so that thus I can remember myself.
> Detached and at ease,
> The eagle will allow me to pass to liberty.]

> Ya me di al poder que a mi destino rige.
> No me agarro ya de nada, para así no tener nada que defender
> No tengo pensamientos, para así poder *ver*.
> No tengo ya nada, para poder así recordarme de mi.
> Sereno y desprendido,
> me dejará el aguila pasar a la libertad.
> (*The Eagle's Gift* 309)

By the same token, recent Spanish mystical poetry shows the influences of the Latin American poets Rubén Darío and Cesar Vallejo, who both explore the theme of impartial love as destiny dictated by higher levels of universal law.

These poets reflect Rielo's style of strength, courage, and power in its originality and purpose. There are, of course, degrees in everything, and Rielo's verse, due to certain special powers of mind generated by the vow of chastity, is the most elevated current model in the mystic tradition. Also it is thinking from the perspective of level or *scale* that gives force to Rielo's poetry; and it is this same thinking that is often lacking in great contemporary critics like Jacques Derridá in his synthesis of deconstruction. The principle of *scale* is lacking in Derridá's analyses of both "differential mysticism" and "logocentric mysticism."

Rielo's message is that we do not understand love as a positive emotion, an emotion, that is, for which there is no opposite and so no inner contradictions. It would be another matter if the opposite of self-love (the me, what is mine, vanity, pride, and ego) were self-hate. In Rielo's symbol, however, "Yes" as verb, noun, and adjective has no such opposite; the "fruition" attracts no contrary, since it unites everything in itself as one. It is a unification, a *desposado*, [marriage] of opposites--a third thing or "*tercio incluso*" that we do not know because we swing from one side to the other like bells.

Self-love is built on an illusion called imagination in the language of psychology and consequently is not real. Both personality and all negative emotions are based on self-love, and these must be overcome in the first stage of the "sacrifice of mechanical suffering" mentioned earlier. As Christ puts it, "If any man cometh unto me and hateth not his own father, mother and children and brethern and sisters, yea and his own life also, he cannot be my disciple" (Lk 14:26). In Greek the word translated as "his own life" means "soul" or "psyche." Thus, hating one's own life or one's own soul is equivalent to hating the elements in oneself that are controlled by self-love. The soul at the level of ordinary experience is a point of intense self-love which we take as constitutive of our individual identity; when self-love is interfered with, personality comes into automatic action and we hate. Rielo's pure-symbol "Yes," on the other hand, reveals the true, essential emotions of awe and love--emotions that transcend self-interest.

To complete the presentation of Rielo's vision of the genetic conception of love, the important role of Mary the Virgin Mother of Christ in Rielo's poetry must be defined. The Virgin Mary is Third Force, the mediator between man and Christ, just as Christ is the mediator between man and God. In one of Rielo's most beautiful sonnets we read:

[How many times, Mary, has my consciousness been
attacked by the devil, and how much numancian[7]
resistance have I liberated before his undivine hatred.
Well you know I tell you in filial confidence.

Satan hurls my body, nailing it in agony,
to the fire, to the water, to the mud... with snake apron

---

7.   The Spaniards' resistance to a foreign invasion that would attempt to compromise the country's idiosyncrasy is expressed by various authors through the Numancia myth. This myth acquires a truly transcendent relevance with the historical evocation of this Spanish city's heroic resistance to the Roman blockade, a resistance that lasted until, all resources exhausted, the Numancians decided to throw themselves to the fire. The Spanish essayist J.L. Abellán calls the "Myth of Numancia the great tragedy of liberty" (Rielo, ¿Existe...? 45).

and his vomit overflows in my morning of love
fleeing from my sob with infernal violence.

I make you the confessor of my sad agony.
Grasp with your hands my hard suffering in flight.
and never leave me, no, because in strong dual

of guilt and innocence goes my life
and because it is certain doubt if I have offended God,
I have of you the Grace that always has been mine.]

Cuántas veces, María, ha sido mi conciencia
por el diablo atacada, y cuánto numantino
resistir he librado frente a su oído indivino.
Bien sabes te lo digo en filial confidencia.

Satán mi cuerpo arroja, clavándolo en dolencia,
al fuego, al agua, al lodo... con arpón viperino
y revierte su vómito en mi amor matutino
huyendo de mi llanto con infernal violencia.

Te hago la confesora de mi triste agonía.
Acoge con tus manos mi dura pena en vuelo
y no me dejes nunca, no, porque en fuerte duelo

de culpable o inocente vase esta vida mía.
Y porque es duda cierta si he a Dios ofendido,
tengo de ti que siempre la gracia me haya sido.

(Sombras vírgenes n. pag.)

In the ancient Gnostic manuscripts called the *Nag Hammadi*, the language is even more practical and clear in its imagery. In the secret book of John in the Gnostic gospels we read:

> "Yet again, a third time, I went forth;
> I am the light that dwells in light.
> I am the remembrance of Forethought.
> I intended to enter the middle of darkness and the
> center of the underworld. I brightened my face with
> light from the consummation of this world, and entered
> the middle of this prison, the prison of the body.
> "I said, 'let whosoever hears arise from

deep sleep'. 'A sleeper wept and shed bitter
tears. Wiping them away, the sleeper said,
'who is calling my name? What is the source of
this hope that has come to me, dwelling in
the bondage of prison?'
"I said,

> 'I am the Forethought of pure Light.
> I am the Thought of the virgin Spirit,
> > who has raised you to a place of honor.

> > Arise,
> > Remember that you have heard,
> > and trace your root:
> > > for I am compassionate.
> > Guard yourself against the angel of
> > misery, the demons of chaos, and
> > all who entrap you,
> > and beware of deep sleep, and the
> > trap at the center of the underworld!

"I raised the sleeper, and sealed the sleeper in
luminous water with five seals, that death might not
prevail from that moment on."
"Behold, now I shall ascend to the perfect realm.
I have finished discussing everything with you. I
have told you everything, for you to record and
communicate secretly to your spiritual friends. For
this is the mystery of the unshakable race."
The savior communicated these things to
John for him to record and safeguard. He said
to him, "cursed is everyone who will trade these
things for a present, for food, drink, clothes or
> > anything else."
These things were communicated to John as a
mystery, and afterward the Savior disappeared
at once. Then John went to the other disciples and
reported what the savior had told him.
> Jesus Christ
> > Amen
> > (*Secret Teachings* 86-87)

These teachings are called "secret" (that is, esoteric) by Christ
himself in the manuscript. The "remembrance of forethought" is the

act of "remembering oneself" before reacting mechanically; it is the quality of knowing and attentive awareness of thought as thought *only*. The "light that dwells in light" is the consciousness of Being as God that lies within ordinary consciousness. The path to this consciousness of Being is inward and can only be followed if one escapes from the prison of the body. The "sleeper" is man not yet evolved in consciousness, with no unified "I," no freedom, no will. The "sleeper" lives what Ortega y Gasset calls *alteración*, and, to awaken, must trace his root--the "compassion", conscious impartial love that Rielo calls *congenitud*. The forces that hold the "sleeper" in bondage are negative emotions learned through imitation and injury to the ego, the unreal aspect of man created by life. At the collective level these forces create a demonic chaos: the multiplicity of many egos, each following its own material desires. The biggest enemy is "deep sleep" or the "trap," which is the *illusion* of being already in possession of full consciousness. The luminous water in which the "sleeper" is sealed is the enlightened emotional center (water in traditional symbolism meaning emotion and life).

From the perspective of the Derridian theory of *differànce*, and from the perspective of differential mysticism, my critical synthesis is as follows: Fernando Rielo was born the 28th of August, making his astrological sign Virgo (the Virgin), the sixth house of the Zodiac. This sign "is ruled by Mercury, the planet of reason, expression and dexterity. The mercurial disposition infused by this sign provides changes ... of environment and therefore new associates and friendship are constantly being formed.... It is said, and with considerable truth, that love is blind for were one to see faults in the beloved one the master *passion* would never find expression. Therefore the children of Virgo..." (Heindel 128). Rielo is a Virgo whose *sign* in pure-symbol is the *Virgen Santísima* [Most Holy Virgin]. The poet's use of the ancient Spanish lexicon is infused with esoteric astrology by means of the differential forces of non-definiteness and context (Derridá, "White mythology"). In the tenth sonnet of *Sombras vírgenes*, we find the pure-symbol *signified* as "Virginante aurora." This expression takes the pre-existing concept of the Virgin and combines it with the progressive verbal aspect marker *nante [*-ing] to form "virgining" (a special musical quality derives from the accent that falls on the vowel *a* in the Spanish *"Virginante"*). "Aurora" expands from translation "Dawn" to take in the mystical *aurora borealis*, the lights at the far north of the globe of Earth. Thus these mysterious lights of dawn are "virgining," gaining the powerful higher energy of the sex force. Or, as Rielo puts it:

202

[Let nothing come that is not of You
to my night shadowing itself in Finite
that is put out by undefinable goodbye
of a light that I loved so very much.

And my window to the sea almost asleep
coil quickly its horizon
and suspended it holds me in the distance
where my death explodes and no one hears it.

Rapid flight, rapid light ... ecstasy,
quick rapture that seals us my kiss
and yours: unreturnable, divine, unique...

You, Christ, with the Father in truth you are
the virgining incorruptible lights of Dawn.
Far from time and far from its footprint!]

Que nada venga que de Ti no sea
a mi noche sombreándose en finito
que se apaga de adiós indefinible
por una luz a la que tanto amé.

Y mi ventana al mar casi dormida
enrolle presurosa su horizonte
y suspenso me quede en la distancia

donde mi muerte estalle y nadie la oiga.
Súbito vuelo, súbita luz... rapto,
súbito rapto que nos selle mi ósculo
con el tuyo: irregreso, divino, único...

Tú, Cristo, con el Padre en verdad eres
la virginante aurora incorruptible.
¡Qué más lejos del tiempo y de su huella!
                          (*Sombras vírgenes* n. pag.)

One notes in Rielo's use of pure-symbol a rare power not often
encountered in poetry. Salvador de Madariaga in his essay "The
Genius of Spain" describes this rare power in the Spanish language as
"difficult to define, a kind of genius for direct utterance which enables

it to attain great emotional or spiritual effects by means of daily, humble words, expressive of daily humble ideas, precisely that poetic quality--it will be recognized--which Wordsworth strove all his life to acquire.... A language which can be at the same time so bare and so beautiful is a great national spirit. And thus, even if no other facts were available, a study of Spanish poetry would be sufficient to establish that though Spain may not be in the front rank of political and economic powers, she undoubtedly is one of the great spiritual powers of the world" (14). This great spiritual heritage in language derives from the extraordinary mixture of languages in Spanish civilization, which as Madariaga points out began in Galicia, Asturias, León, and Castile, the areas least affected by the Romanization of the Peninsula (the eastern and southern regions, by contrast, fell under heavy Roman influence and later were held under the domination of the Moorish Arabs until 1492).

The range of musical possibilities in Spanish far outstrips that of the other Romance languages. The special power of the Spanish language in itself must be remembered as one explores the lyrical qualities and powerful message of Rielo's contemporary mystical poetry. The unity of theme and symbol forged through the *Poe'S* could not be accomplished in any other language. Rielo has stated that Spain is essentially mystic. I maintain that the mystical is also inherent in its language. In Rielo's sonnets the mystical nature of Spanish language and its "rare power," as described by Madariaga, are *felt* as energy. Matter is indistinguishable from energy, the two forming a manifestation of the one reality, as in the Christian teaching that in the beginning was God and the world was *created* by him. In Oriental philosophy there is always a clear distinction between *creation of shape and form* and the *creation of the substance* of these shapes and forms (Ramacharaka 102-3).

Considered non-logocentrically, from the perspective of Derridian *déroulement*, Rielo's pure-symbol raises to its own level transverberating energy. In such energy operate the two sacred, aesthetically intentional laws of creation: *la treidad* or the law of three, and *ingenitud*[8] or the law of seven. Such energy is figured by the highest connotative signifiers of the *out of oneself*: *luz* (the speed of light), *vuelo* (high flight). Rielo points out that "Christ transcends adoration in such

---

8. Ingenitud is a neologism that turns the adjective for "unbegotten" or "not yet created" into a noun: "unbornness," "uncreatedness."

a degree that it is purified by a love that makes Him one with divine love. This adoration cancels by love all forms of primitive cults in which "servitude" is the tribute with which the human being pays God. The textual words of Christ, "I do not call you now servants..., you I have called friends because all I have heard from my Father..." constitute the highest and truthfully magnificent mysticism" ("*Dos intérpretes...*" 13). Thus love empowers man, infusing the energy of the one reality into desire for Being.

The following sonnet takes as its theme Christ's saying, "**I am** the Resurrection and the Life":

[Universe in me does not exist nor do I know if yesterday I had it open to my senses: nothing I affirm of my soul.
I don't know what has happened to me. Can it be empty space of
calm?
Or is it your blood in my blood that sacramented I acquired?

My world is another world: ascending from love into love
with height on height suffering that barefoot love unites.
My coagulated yesterday, of sky will be palm.
Certain of my venture, cover me last cloud

let death untie, thirsty lovedeath.
Only you are fountain that creates life in my life,
life that You transcend and in You thirstless rests.

Oh, freshness of watered garden that breaths my soul
with your water newlywed and Your being in my wound
until at last healed in You, Christ, I may rest!]

No existe mundo en mí ni sé si ayer lo tuve
abierto a mis sentidos: nada afirmo de mi alma.
No sé qué me ha pasado. ¿Será vacío en calma?
¿O es tu sangre en mi sangre que sacramentada obtuve?

Mi mundo es otro mundo: de amor en amor sube
con alta en alta pena que amor descalzo ensalma.
Mi coagulado ayer, del cielo será palma.
Cierto de mi ventura, cúbreme última nube

que la muerte disuelve, muerte de amor sedienta.
Sólo tú eres la fuente que da vida a mi vida,
vida que Tú transciendes y en Ti sin sed remanse.

¡Oh frescor de regado huerto que a mi alma alienta
con tu agua desposado y estarte así en mi herida
hasta que al fin curada en Ti, Cristo, descanse!
(Sombras virgenes n. pag.)

Faith is the motif and counterpoint of the main theme of "love-death" or *Liebestraum*, as in Richard Wagner's musical rendition. The faith of understanding is Rielo's *signified* and love-death the *signifier*. Hope and love are feelings that, when activated by the Third Force, become impulses, and without these impulses faith is not possible. Faith is our state of being in the present moment. This faith requires ascetic purification through struggle with the desires of the body. Faith is the positive emotion of the awakened higher emotional center, an emotion that produces consciousness. One has to *renacer* [be reborn] on a higher psychological level. Rielo uses imagery drawn from nature as a pure-symbol referring to man's life and his being. Faith enables comprehension of the spirit of nature reflected in man through the teachings of Jesus Christ. Rielo's mystical language is a language of symbols in exact concordance with the laws of conscious Being, a language that through *congenitud* can move and change both the reader and his material reality. Pure-poetry, in Rielo's own words, is the highest form of communication: the communication of peace.

The "kiss" in Rielian symbology is the sensation of the mouth becoming "light" for the whole of the body: light, attention, sensation become *one*. The miracle of Christ in the Resurrection is the sensitivity of the body to the light of intentional sensation. The lip is open to connect with the forces of the universe: "my universe is another universe." In the Grace of God lies the *desire* to be: "passion." The etymology of the word "passion" relates it to suffering; thus the theme of the poem: love-death.

As this study began with a quotation from Fernando Rielo Pardal, poet, mystic, and modern hero, it is proper to end it with his words as well:

[I contemplate, Christ, in dreamed heart
that faith is prayerful miracle of the believer,
no method or calculated discourse
to reach you in his life ascendent.

Miracle makes the damaged heart
near to our stricken breath.
Touch me, my Christ, and I ectatic
move away like You from an absent sun.

Make with my nomadic faith the mountain
and let my yesterday burn with the fire
and free my weedless wheat fields.

You created me with your hand for watering,
hand of sob that moistens my sob.
Let it alone remain... that you take me next!]

Contemplo, Cristo, en corazón soñado
que fe es milagro orante del creyente,
no método o discurso calculado
para alcanzarte en su vida ascendente.

El milagro hace al corazón dañado
prójimo de nuestro hálito doliente.
Tócame, Cristo mío, y yo extasiado
me aleje como Tú de un sol ausente.

Haz con mi fe nómada la montaña
y que mi ayer se queme con el fuego
y campeen mis trigales sin cizaña.

Me creaste con tu mano para el riego,
mano de llanto que a mi llanto empaña.
¡Que sólo quede... que me lleves luego!
(*Sombras vírgenes* n. pag.)

The mystery of the world is thus illuminated and the darkness of
the interior world reveals the galaxies, the planets, the sun within the
poet's own body. The true sun is the sun of his own heart that radiates
faith and conscious love, in exact accordance with God's perfect laws.

WORKS CITED

Alonso, Dámaso. Letter to José María López Sevillano. Mar. 10, 1979.

---. *Poetas españoles contemporáneos.* Madrid: Gredos, 1969.

Andreu, Blanca. *Báculo de Babel.* Madrid: Ediciones Hiperión, 1983.

---.*De una niña de provincias que se vino a vivir en un Chagall.* 5th ed. Madrid: Hiperión, 1986.

Anglada, Francisco. "La voz poética de Fernando Rielo" Nueva Andalucía [Seville, Spain], 12 Jan. 1978: 13.

Arbo, Juan Sebastián. *Cervantes.* Barcelona: Editorial Noguer, 1956.

Asensio y Toledo, José María. *Cervantes y sus obras.* Sevilla; Spain: J.M. Geofrin, 1870.

Azaña y Díez, Manuel. *La invención del "Quijote", y otros ensayos.* Madrid, Espasa-Calpe. 1934.

Bell, Aubrey. *Cervantes.* Norman, OK: U of Oklahoma P, 1947.

Benardete, José & Angel Flores. *Cervantes Across the Centuries.* New York: Dryden Press, 1947.

---. *Anatomy of Don Quijote.* Ithaca: Cornell UP, 1932.

Betanzos Palacios, Odón. Introduction. *Balcón a la bahía.* By Fernando Rielo. Constantine, Sevilla: FFR, 1989. 5-9.

Brenan, Gerald. *The Literature of the Spanish People*. Cambridge: Cambridge UP, 1962.

Busoño, Carlos. *Invasión de la realidad*. Madrid: Espasa Calpe, 1962.

Butler, Edward Cuthbert. *Western Mysticism: The teaching of Augustine, Gregory & Bernard on contemplation and the contemplative life*. 3rd ed. New York: Barnes & Noble, 1968.

Castañeda, Carlos. *The Eagle's Gift*. New York: Simon & Schuster, 1981.

Chandler, Richard and Kessel Schwartz. *A New History of Spanish Literature*. Baton Rouge: Louisiana State U P, 1961.

Church, Margaret. *Don Quixote*. New York: New York U P, 1971.

Close, Anthony. *The Romantic Approach to Don Quixote*. Cambridge: Cambridge UP, 1978.

Couffon, Claude. Introduction. *Dieu et arbre*. By Fernando Rielo. Trans. Claude Couffon. Paris: Caractères, 1985. 7-11.

A Critical New Testament. (Greek and English) New York: Wiley, 1977.

Derridá, Jacques. *Of Grammatology*. Trans. Gayatri C. Spivak. Baltimore: Johns Hopkins UP, 1976.

---. "White Mythology." *Margins of Philosophy*. Chicago: Chicago UP, 1982.

Eckhart, Meister. *A modern translation*. Trans. Bernard Blakney. New York: Harper & Row, 1941.

Emerson, Ralph Waldo. *Miscellanies*. London: Macmillan, 1884.

Entwistle, William James. *Cervantes*. Oxford: Clarendon Press, 1940.

Fitzmaurice-Kelly, James. *Miguel de Cervantes Saavedra, a Memoir* Oxford: The Clarendon Press, 1973

Fontes. *Narrativi de San Ignatio*. II Vols. Ediciones MHSI: Rome, 1943.

Ford, Jeremiah and Ruth Lansing. *Cervantes: A Tentative Bibliography*. Cambridge, Mass: Harvard U P, 1931.

Forés, Aldo R. *La poesía mística de Fernando Rielo*. New York: Senda Nueva de Ediciones, 1985.

Gazarian-Gautier, Marie Lise. Back cover. *Llanto azul* By Ferando Rielo. Smithtown, New York: Exposition P, 1980.

Green, otis Howard. *The Literary Mind of Medieval and Renaissance Spain*. Lexington: Kentucky U P, 1970.

Grismer, Raymond. *Cervantes: A Bibliography*. New York: The H.W. Wilson Company. 1946.

Gurdjieff, G.I. *All and Everything: Beelzebub's Tales to his Grandson*. E.P. Dutton: New York, 1978.

Guthrie, Kenneth Sylvan. *Plotinus, the complete works*. II vols. London: George Bell and Sons, 1918.

Hammarskjöld, Dag. *Markings*. Trans. Leif Fjöberg and W. H. Auden. New York: Alfred A. Knopf, 1974.

Hatzfeld, Helmut. *Estudios literarios sobre la mística española*. Madrid: Editorial Gredos, 1968.

Heidegger, Martin. *Being and Time*. Trans. John MacQuarrie and Edward Robinson. London: SCM Press, 1962.

Heindel, M. and A.F. *The Message of the Stars*. London: Fowler, 1973.

Hiriart, Rosario. *La mirada poética de José García Nieto*. Barcelona, Spain: Editorial Icaria, 1990.

James, William. *Collected Essays and Reviews*. London: Longmans, Green, 1920.

Jiménez, José Olivio. *Diez años de poesía española (1960-1970)* Madrid: Insula, 1972.

Lagos, Ramiro. "Critiques", *Llanto azul* by Fernando Rielo. Smithtown, New York: Exposition P, 1980. 121-122.

López Ferreiro, A. *Historia de la Santa A.M. Iglesia de Santiago de Compostela*. 2 vols. Santiago de Compostela: Salvora, 1983.

López Sevillano, José M. Introduction. *Llanto azul* by Fernando Rielo. Smithtown, New York: Exposition P, 1980. ix-xxi.

---. "Pure metaphysics in Fernando Rielo." Fernando Rielo: poeta y filósofo/Poet and Philosopher. Constantina (Sevilla), Spain: FFR, 1990. 201-213.

---. "The Passage of Spanish Mysticism into the Novel." Fernando Rielo: poeta y filósofo/Poet and Philosopher. Constantina (Sevilla), Spain: FFR, 1990. 149-164.

---. Prologue. *Pasión y muerte* by Fernando Rielo. Madrid: Ornigraf R. Arsango, 1979. 5-13.

Madariaga, Salvador. *Guía del lector del Quijote*. Madrid: Editorial Sudamericana, 1972.

---. *The Genius of Spain and Other Essays on Spanish Contemporary Literature*. Oxford: Clarendon Press, 1923.

Martí, Alama. Introductory Speech. Agrupación Literaria Amigos de la Poesía. Valencia. 7 June 1979.

Menendez Pidal, Ramón. *Cervantes y Lope de Vega*. 6th ed. Madrid: Espasa-Calpe, 1964.

Moseley, William. *Spanish Literature 1500-1700*. Westport, Connecticut: Greenwood Press, 1984.

Navarro Tomás, Tomás. Introduction. *Las Moradas* by Santa Teresa. Madrid: Espasa-Calpe, 1962. v-xv.

Nida, Eugene Albert. *Language Structure and Translation.* Stanford, California: Stanford University Press, 1975.

Nieto, José García. *Las mil mejores poesías de la lengua castellana.* 27 ed. Madrid: Clásicos Bergua. 1984. 717.

---. *Del campo y soledad.* Madrid: Colección Adonáis. Num xxv. 1946.

Ortega y Gasset, José. *The Self and the Other.* Trans. William R. Trask. New York: Dial, 1952.

Ouspensky, Peter D. *The Fourth Way.* New York: Alfred A Knopf, 1959.

Ouspensky, Peter D. *In Search of the Miraculous: Fragments of an unknown teaching.* New York, Harcourt, Brace. 1949.

Panero, Leopoldo. *Obras completas.* Madrid: Editora Nacional, 1973.

Petacchi. *Work for Being in the Machine Age.* New York: Philosophical library, 1980.

Petraglia Aguirre, Hugo. Introduction. *Noche clara* by Fernando Rielo. Madrid: Ornigraf R. Arsango, 1980. 9-17.

Ramacharaka. *Gnani Yoga.* Chicago: Yogi Publication Society, 1934.

Rielo, Fernando. *Balcón a la bahía.* Constantina (Sevilla), Spain: FFR, 1989.

---. "Comentario a un cuestionario." Letter to Dr. Ramiro Lagos. July 3, 1980.

---. "Definición mística del hombre dentro de una concepción metafísica del ser." Unpublished speech. United Nations. 18 Nov. 1980.

---. *Dios y árbol.* Madrid: Ornigraf R. Arsango. 1979.
---. *Dolor entre cristales.* Constantina (Sevilla), Spain: FFR, 1990.

---. "Dos intérpretes de la mística española en el Siglo de Oro: San Juan de la Cruz y San Ignacio de Loyola." *San Juan de la Cruz y San Ignacio de Loyola: Dos polos hispánicos.* Madrid: EDI-6, 1990.

---. *¿Existe una Filosofía española?* Constantina (Sevilla), Spain: FFR, 1990. 97-131.

---. *Raíces y valores historicos del pensamiento español.* Constantina (Sevilla), Spain: FFR, 1988. 140-42.

---. "Introducción a una concepción genética de la poesía." Unpublished speech. Fifth World Congress of Poets. Madrid, July 1982.

---. "Introduction to My Thought". Unpublished essay. 1985.

---. *Llanto azul.* Smithtown, New York: Esposition P, 1980.

---. *Noche clara.* Madrid: Ornigraf R. Arsango, 1980.

---. *Paisaje desnudo.* Madrid: Ornigraf R. Arsango, 1979.

---. *Pasión y muerte.* Madrid: Ornigraf R. Arsango, 1979.

---. "Poesía y mística." *Mystère et matière.* Louvain, Belgium: Quatrième Festival Européen de Poésie. 1982. 27-35.

---. *Sombras vírgenes.* Unpublished ms. 1990.

---. *Teoría del Quijote: Su mística hispánica.* Maryland: Studia humanitatis, 1982.

---. *Theory of Don Quixote: Its Hispanic Mysticism.* Trans. Zelda Brooks. New York: Senda Nueva, 1989.

---. *Transfiguration.* Trans. Bernard Sesé. Paris: Editions Caractères, 1986.

Rilke, Rainer Maria. *Letters to Merline, 1919-1922.* Trans. Violet M. Macdonald. London: Methund, 1951.

213

Río, Angel del. *Historia de la literatura española: Desde sus orígenes hasta 1700.* II Vols. New York: Holt, Rinehart & Winston, 1963.

Saint Bonaventure. *De reductione artium ad theologiam.* Trans. Sister Emma Therese Healy. 2nd Edition. New York: Franciscan institute, Saint Bonaventure U P, 1955.

San Juan de la Cruz. *Vida y obras de San Juan de la Cruz.* Madrid: BAC, 1973.

Santa Teresa de Jesús. *Las Moradas.* Madrid: Espasa-Calpe, 1962.

---. *Santa Teresa de Jesús: Obras Completas.* 2nd Ed. Madrid: BAC, 1967.

Schevill, Rudolph. *Cervantes.* New York: Duffield & Company, 1919.

Scott, Walter., Ed and trans. *Hermetica* Oxford: Oxford UP, 1924.

The Secret Teachings of Jesus: Four Gnostic Gospels. Trans. Marvin W. Meyer. New York: Random House, 1984

Simms, Edna. "The Mystical Meditative Content of Fernando Rielo's '*Llanto azul*'": Fernando Rielo: poeta y filósofo/ Poet and Philosopher.. Constantina (Sevilla), Spain: FFR, 1991. 51-61.

Steiner, George. *Language and Silence.* New York: Atheneum, 1967.

Torbert, Eugene Charles. *Cervantes' Place Names. A lexicon* Metuchen, NJ: Scarecrow Press, 1978.

Torres Marín, Francisco. "En torno a la portada". *Noche clara* by Fernando Rielo. Madrid: Ornigraf R. Arsango, 1980. 5-8.

Venegas, Adolfo. "La mística contemporánea". *El Pueblo* [Arequipa, Perú] 19 May 1979:9.

Villoslada, Ricardo García. *San Ignacio de Loyola: Nueva biografía.* Madrid: BAC, 1986.

Watts, Henry Edward. *Miguel de Cervantes: His Life and Works.* London: Adam & Charles Black, 1895.

Webster's New World Dictionary of. American Eng. 3rd ed. 1988.

Wilson, Edward Meryon. *Spanish and English Literature of the 16th and 17th Centuries.* Cambridge: Cambridge U P, 1980.

Yeats, W.B. *Collected Poems.* New York: Macmillan, 1951.

Scripta Humanistica

Directed by
BRUNO M. DAMIANI
The Catholic University of America
COMPREHENSIVE LIST OF PUBLICATIONS*

67. *Other Voices: Essays on Italian Regional Culture and Language*. Ed. John Staulo. $35.50
68. Mario Aste, *Grazia Deledda: Ethnic Novelist*. $38.50
69. Edward C. Lynskey, *The Tree Surgeon's Gift*. Foreword by Fred Chappell. $22.50
70. Henry Thurston-Griswold, *El idealismo sintético de Juan Valera*. Prólogo por Lee Fontanella. $44.50
71. Mechthild Cranston, *Laying Ways*. Preface by Germaine Brée. $26.50
72. Roy A Kerr, *Mario Vargas Llosa: Critical Essays on Characterization*. $43.50
73. Eduardo Urbina, *Principios y fines del "Quijote"*. $45.00
74. Pilar Moyano, *Fernando Villalón: El poeta y su obra*. Prólogo por Luis Monguió. $46.50
75. Diane Hartunian, *La Celestina: A Feminist Reading of the "carpe diem" Theme*. $45.50
76. Victoria Urbano, *Sor Juana Inés de la Cruz: amor, poesía, soledumbre*. Edición y prólogo de Adelaida López de Martínez. $43.50
77. Magda Graniela-Rodríguez, *El papel del lector en la novela mexicana contemporánea: José Emilio Pacheco y Salvador Elizondo*. $46.50
78. Robert L. Sims, *El primer García Márquez: un estudio de su periodismo de 1948-1955*. $48.00
79. Zelda Irene Brooks, *Poet, Mystic, Modern Hero: Fernando Rielo Pardal*. $49.50
80. *La Celestina*. Edición, introducción y notas by Bruno M. Damiani. $45.00
81. Jean P. Keller, *The Poet's Myth of Fernán González*. $47.50
82. Maksoud Feghali, *Le phénomène de construction et de destruction dans "Le Songe" de Du Bellay*. Preface by Michael J. Giordano. $49.50

BOOK ORDERS

* Clothbound. *All book orders*, except library orders, must be prepaid and addressed to **Scripta Humanistica**, 1383 Kersey Lane, Potomac, Maryland 20854. *Manuscripts* to be considered for publication should be sent to the same address.